Steve Geyer

Shameless

Set Free From the Mask

Word Alive Press
131 Cordite Road, Winnipeg, MB R3W 1S1
www.wordalivepress.ca

Dedication

Ken and Carolyn Drez are the loving parents of Nontie, Mark, Michael, Keri, and Christian and the doting grandparents of eleven grandchildren. Thankfully, they are also the spiritual parents to a countless number of "urchins" like me. Ken and Carolyn effortlessly demonstrate God's amazing grace and unconditional love without having to resort to words. They love with boundaries, yet without walls, and their legacy is secure.

For Harrison Jude Geyer

*I pray that you, my precious little love nugget, may grow
up in grace and love, and be altogether shameless.*

Contents

Acknowledgments

I now fully understand that when someone writes in their acknowledgements, "This book would not have been possible without the following people," the author is not exaggerating or using hyperbole. There really is no way under heaven or above hell you would be reading this book without the love, support, and even constructive butt-kicking from people whom I love and who love me.

Thanks to Eric Spath for being so much more than my manager. You are a longtime, trusted, and dearly beloved friend. You have faithfully advised, guided, challenged, and encouraged me for over twenty years. I value your honesty, integrity, and vulnerability as well as your fierce loyalty and work ethic. But mostly I value that you always speak the truth to me no matter how much I would rather have you tell me fairy tales.

Thank you, Holly Smith, for enduring the way I write and for being gently tough during the editing process. I am grateful for your encouragement, for getting the spirit of this book, and for adding some of the best parts. Of course, I know you'll just want to receive your reward in heaven, so I'll take credit for those parts in this life. And a special thank you to my friend Claudia Debner, who took the time to read this with her orange pen and help me find some better ways of saying things.

Thanks to Doug "Doogie" Jones, not only for our longtime friendship, but also for creating an incredible book cover and design that makes me want to pick it up and take a look inside. "I'm so happy… " (You do know the voice I'm using, right?)

In sports, games are usually won or lost in the ninth inning, fourth quarter, or third period. With that in mind, coaches and managers place the ball or the last shot in the capable hands of a trusted athlete. I'm so grateful for the team at Word Alive Press, who got this book late in the game and delivered when the heat was on. Thanks to Jen Jandavs-Hedlin for her help and making all the artwork "work," and to Evan Braun who has no idea how much his edits, comments, and suggestions not only encouraged me but made me sound a whole lot smarter. Thank you!

I am grateful for the men who, without any trumpets or fanfare, entered my life to provide wise fatherly counsel or brotherly love and some well-timed, loving rebukes when I needed them most: Stephen Mansfield, Don Finto, Alan Robertson, Paul Billington, Jim Davis, Mike Demus, Dee White, Tore Stautland, Eric Spath, Chaz Corzine, Devlin Donaldson, Maury Buchanan, Jack McCarty, Stan Horrell, Don Harris, Tim Royal, Drew Brooks, Matthew Clark, Chris Tanner, Val Akins, Phillip Fields, Ed Richardson, Ken Drez, Bill Geyer, and Graham Geyer. A very special thank you to Don Crossland for getting me started on the journey out from behind the mask.

To my Revive family: Tom, Patty, Mike, Tammi, Cameron, Carol, David, Dolores, Katie, Rolf, Brad, Paul, Carrie, Trey, Betsy, Cammycakes, Zoie, Blake, JackMath, Dustin, Richard, Lorin, Ken, Shannon, Jason, Satoya, Ben, Shawna, Lauren, Ronnie, Dustin, Kiko, Clemi, Kelly, Kristen, Mel, Cody, Wally, Emily, Shelby, Niki, Brooke, Steve, Luke, Ashley, Zack, and Parker. I love you all from the bottom of my pancreas. "Cheese balls & Zzzatarain's baby!"

I am grateful to my mother Barbara "Bobbie" Geyer, who while privately battling her own shame raised three children and instilled in each of us a sense of duty, loyalty, and rightness, as well as the drive to follow our dreams.

I am equally grateful for my sister and brother. Maureen, the person who, for all intents and purposes, practically raised me as a second mom and gave up a lot of her childhood so that I could have one. Bill, for being the best big brother a kid could have, and for encouraging and supporting my comedic aspirations—not to mention fixing my smile and writing some of my best comedy material.

I can't find the words to adequately thank and honor my children, Kirsten and Graham. These two gifts from heaven are the delight of my heart. My most treasured life lessons came from being your dad, and I so appreciate that you let me "grow up" with you guys. The grace and mercy you've extended to this imperfect dad will no doubt reflect in the rewards you will receive from the perfect Father. And to my new daughter-in-love Gracie, you not only gave my son a son, you brought new meaning and a "forever love" into his life.

This book would have not been possible if not for my dearly beloved friend, cheerleader, and eternally youthful helpmate. I owe an immeasurable debt of gratitude to Kathy, who is the bravest, most honorable, and most honest person I've ever known. I'm awed by how you love and protect our children. Your love, fierce loyalty, and ability to laugh like you've never heard my comedy material before makes me want to make you laugh more than any other audience, anywhere… anyhow. You've done more to rescue me from shame than any book, teaching, or seminar by continually walking with me on this journey—out from under shame and into God's marvelous kingdom of light. To quote Dorothy Gale, "I love you most of all."

Preface

"Shame on you!"

I'll grant that starting with that phrase is probably not the most inviting way to get you to keep reading, but it's important to shine the light on shame right up front and keep it from slinking back into the shadows. Shame is one of the most powerful negative forces on earth and probably has more control over your life than you may even realize.

When you read the words—"shame on you"—what voice did you hear? Whose face did you see? That phrase may be so familiar to your ears that you've seen a collage of faces upon reading it. Well, trust me, you are not alone. Most of us have at some level dealt with shame. Over the last fifteen years, I have been kept more than busy ministering to people controlled by shame, all while fighting my own secret battle with it.

So to anyone who has ever despised or cursed the face in the mirror, exited a room full of people and immediately began assailing themselves for being worthless and stupid, or felt that they will always be the last one picked for kickball, I extend to you my deepest empathy and heartfelt compassion, because I know what it's like. It's not easy battling an invisible enemy. You have no clue where the attack is coming from and no sense of direction in which to fight back. Your family and friends may not understand what's the matter with you, because you don't even know what's wrong with you. Something is definitely wrong, but it may not be you.

What's wrong may be something that's been a part of your life for so long (even beginning in childhood) that it just feels normal. Feelings of self-loathing, in all its various forms, should never feel normal. But negative thoughts and feelings can become so familiar that the only time we feel normal is when the previously mentioned invisible enemy is present.

For most of my life I waged a losing battle with this invisible enemy and was convinced that I—and I alone—was the only person who did. After fifteen years in pastoral ministry and countless experiences as a touring speaker and comedian, I discovered that I was not the only person who was suffering. In fact, I was at first shocked and then saddened to learn how many people battle this invisible foe.

What started out as a five-hundred-word blog in October 2013 has morphed into a book of nearly seventy thousand words! Each time I would write my concluding thought or insight, another thought or insight would be there waiting to be included. It was October 2014 when I realized I was woefully past submitting this blog by its deadline.

Not so ironically, and rather predictably, during the writing process my invisible foe was ubiquitous in making its presence known and launching more than a few attacks. It got to the point where I couldn't write for days, which turned into weeks and then into months. I couldn't or wouldn't even look at what I had written and fought the urge to delete the whole (insert your expletive of choice) thing.

Fortunately I have an invisible Friend who is more powerful than any foe. Through and abiding in this invisible Friend, I found the strength and courage I needed to continue writing, and then to rewrite entire chapters. My Friend provided me with a loving and encouraging wife, a manager who believed in this project, and an amazingly insightful (and patient) editor. And because of the children my Friend entrusted me with, and a new little love nugget named Jude, I was able to battle on and get to a stopping point. There is so much more that I could write, but maybe after reading this book, you will be the one to write the rest.

The title of the blog was originally *The Invisible War*, but there was already a movie by that name. Then it was changed to *The Secret Battle*, but a book already held that title. When I finally settled on *Shameless*, I discovered there was a TV series with the same name! So I thought, "What the heck?" I'm just going to keep what I settled on… *Shameless*.

So for everyone who curses the mirror, second-guesses everything they say or do, and believes they deserve to be picked last for kickball, I offer to you, *Shameless: Set Free from the Mask*.

Introduction

Some people might question why a comedian would write a book about shame. Some might suppose that shame is the premise for a comedy routine, and we'll all have a good laugh at the end of each chapter. Or if I'm really good at suspense, the laugh will come at the very end of the book. Well, I am a comedian and naturally bent—warped, some might say—toward finding the humor in all situations. I've been accused of turning funerals into parties, parties into funerals, and in some situations I'm known for my skills at ignoring the pink elephant in the room. This ability to avoid or ignore seemed to come naturally, but it was also a learned and developed behavior.

I've been doing stand-up comedy since 1976 (you can thank, or not thank, Danny Campos for this), and for most of my career I was deeply entrenched in what I can only describe as hand-to-hand combat with a spirit (or manifestation) of shame. Ironically, the more I battled shame inwardly, the funnier I was outwardly. I could turn gut-wrenching experiences and memories into comedy routines that would have people laughing and crying at the same time. Who knew that my pain, put on display, would lead to traveling the world, a recording contract, and working with some of the biggest names in the mainstream and Christian entertainment industry? Who knew that for a large part of my career, the audience was unwittingly my own version of group therapy?

I can honestly say that until just a few years ago, I never felt that I belonged or deserved to be onstage, much less in front of an audience. I believed that being on stage was some sort of fluke or cosmic mistake. However, when I was a little boy, I always—and I do mean always—daydreamed, imagined, and fancied myself on stage in front of an audience telling jokes. Looking back I now understand that I was destined to be onstage, but not for reasons I desired. It was for purposes of the One who directs my steps even though I charted my own course. So what happened between being an imaginative, wide-eyed little boy and becoming a grown man with self-serving, misguided feelings, and beliefs? In a word, shame.

Shame is a powerful and shadowy force. It has the power to not only affect you, but also everyone around you. Shame can lead you to think, believe, and behave in ways that are secretive, unhealthy, self-defeating, and self-destructive. Shame can also be very frustrating to everyone you interact with, especially those you love and who loves you.

A Disclaimer

This book contains some insights and lessons I've learned over many years of battling the shadowy force of shame. This is not a how-to or self-help book, it's a collection of experiences and life lessons that I have shared with people over the years in private and classroom settings. The response has always been the same: "When are you going to write a book about this?" So that is what you are holding in your hands—an answer to many requests.

I've always been hesitant to do so, as I am not a psychologist, psychiatrist, nor licensed therapist. There are no letters that precede my name (except for maybe "Mr."), nor after. Though I use terminology that may give you the impression that I have a degree of some sort, I want to clarify right off the bat, I don't! There. That was another manifestation of my victorious walk out from under shame and its effect on my life. I wish to inform, not teach; to inspire, not preach; and to put words to how you might feel, so you can explore and finally speak the language of your heart.

At this point I'd like to let you in on something. I rarely finish reading books like this! Usually halfway through a book, it seems, at least to me, that the second half is just a needless rehash of the first half. I tried not to do that with this book and utilize repetition only to reinforce the truth where we may have believed a lie. And since I have a very short attention span and have genuinely been diagnosed with Attention Deficit Hyperactivity Disorder (ADHD), I want to finish writing this book before I lose interest in it.

For me not to get bored and be true to how God hardwired me, I have written this with the intent to be humorous at times, to provide moments of levity while dealing with some difficult and often painful issues.

Since this is meant to be conversational and storytelling format, I hope that you will hear my voice as you read, and that by putting words or names to some of the feelings I've battled with, it will help you identify with similar feelings you may have had… or still have. Hopefully, this identification process will give you the power to address issues of shame head-on.

Let's get started!

1.

So You'll Know Where I'm Coming From

AFTER SPEAKING AT A LARGE CONFERENCE, I WALKED OFF THE STAGE AND OVER TO WHERE one of my mentors was standing in the wings. I was enjoying the lingering applause as I stood next to him, expecting to hear some words of affirmation for a job well done. Though I never spoke a word, my body language was screaming, *So whataya think? Huh? That was pretty grand, right?* He discerned my desire for affirmation—or, to be more candid, my desire for his approval and verbal applause. He gently placed his arm around my shoulders, drew me close, and said softly, "Wow... you sure do know a lot."

The word *know* hung in the air like a heavy mist while simultaneously piercing my heart like a rapier sword. It felt heavy yet precise. I knew in an instant what he meant and he didn't have to say another word, but he did. And I'm forever grateful. He continued, "You know, Steve, it's somewhat unbecoming to stand in front of people and tell them what you know. It's much more lovely to tell people what you're learning."

As you continue to read, I hope you will remember this encounter, as it is the inspiration and intention for not only *what* I wrote, but also *how* I wrote it. I wrote this book more as a student rather than a teacher.

It's said that most people's greatest fear is to stand up in front of an audience and deliver a speech, and boy can I relate. When I first started doing stand-up comedy, and for many years thereafter, I couldn't eat anything on the day of a performance because of the butterflies, or as I used to call them, the "condors" in my stomach. I don't wish to be gross or gratuitous, but it was not unusual for me to vomit prior to walking onstage in comedy clubs. But walk onstage I did, night after gruesome night. Something compelled me to get up in front of a group of people I didn't know and risk immediate and wholesale rejection.

Doing stand-up comedy in nightclubs is unlike singing a song, performing in a play, or doing a recitation where the audience has until the end to approve or disapprove. In the stand-up comedy world, you've got less than ten seconds before you get your first approval or disapproval. And at times it can be truly gruesome. In music, theater, and other performing arts, a wrong note, missed cue, or botched line can be absorbed among the band, the cast, or over time. Not so with stand-up. Every "miss" that a comic makes is in plain view of the audience, and there is no one else to blame. And every comic will tell you that there are nights when you'd give anything for the floor to swallow you up.

So why would someone so insecure, so afraid of being embarrassed, and so desperate for acceptance from others do such a crazy thing? Why? Because my desire to be accepted overpowered my fear of being rejected. As gruesome as it is to "miss" doing stand-up, it pales in comparison to the exhilaration of when you "hit."

I've learned that shame affects people differently. Some people will turn inward and isolate while others will turn outward and not be able to stand being alone. Some pursue success while some give up. Shame manifests itself in a variety of ways because each of us is unique and very different from everyone else—and not just because of our fingerprints. We have unique and different personalities and grew up in unique and different environments. It's my belief that we are uniquely hardwired by a loving God who created us in His image. Some will seek acceptance wherever they can find it, while others will simply accept or even embrace rejection as their lot in life.

If we don't learn how to respond in a healthy way to shame, there will always be collateral damage. Why? Because whether you choose to outrun shame by being successful, gregarious, and loved by all or simply shut down to avoid any responsibility that may lead to success and keep everyone at arm's length, so they can't hurt you... either way, you still have to face the face in the mirror. And what you say to that face will always outweigh what anyone else says or thinks about you.

I guess you figured out my choice. Yep. My choice was to outrun shame as hard and fast as I could. The problem was that I'm not that fast, and I got really tired—so tired, in fact, that in 2003 I began taking the opposite approach... to just give in and give up. It was during that period that the only parts of the Bible I could relate to were in the book of Job.

Because of a wager to which Satan challenged God, Job became the unwitting player in a test of faithfulness. The bet was that Job would ultimately curse God if He would allow Satan to rob Job of every blessing he had, including his health, wealth, and even his family. God, knowing everything, accepted the terms and so began Job's torment. I'm certain that shame showed up many times during the test, but Job was able to resist shame's influence. What resonated in me were some of the things Job said while he suffered. These words were strangely comforting to me:

> *…so I have been allotted months of futility, and nights of misery have been assigned to me. When I lie down I think, "How long before I get up?" The night drags on, and I toss and turn until dawn.*
>
> —Job 7:3–4

Wow! That's in the Bible? Why isn't that verse on a refrigerator magnet? I was gob-smacked that someone in the Bible had verbalized my feelings. I was intrigued enough to read on.

> *My days are swifter than a weaver's shuttle, and they come to an end without hope.*
>
> —Job 7:6

Hey… my days seem to end without hope too!

> *Therefore I will not keep silent; I will speak out in anguish of my spirit, I will complain in the bitterness of my soul.*
>
> —Job 7:11

Hey, I'm bitter, too… and I like to complain. And heck, I even like to blame!

> *When I think my bed will comfort me and my couch will ease my complaint, even then you frighten me with dreams and terrify me with visions, so that I prefer strangling and death, rather than this body of mine.*
>
> —Job 7:13–15

Hold the phone. You know, Job, I've been having nights when I can't get to sleep, followed by mornings when I can't seem to get out of bed and days when my couch won't let me go. And when I'm awake, I've been having thoughts, too…

> *I despise my life; I would not live forever. Let me alone; my days have no meaning.*
>
> —Job 7:16

I don't know if Job was looking into a mirror when he said these things, but I have said similar things to my mirror. Maybe you have too. I doubt very much that you or I are on the devil's hit list of people to challenge God to another wager, but I do know what's it's like to hate my life and to *"prefer strangling and death."* I also know where my relief and help come from. And to be perfectly frank, I was actually quite surprised that within the pages of the Bible were verses that put words to the feelings I was experiencing in 2003.

Unlike those who are afraid of delivering a speech before an audience, my greatest fear (other than sharks) was the thought of writing this book. Not only because this would require solitude and quiet to collect and then write my thoughts, but also because some people might hate it. Worse than a joke that doesn't get a laugh one night is a book that could very well be a gruesome reminder of a "miss." But the exhilaration that this might help even one person is worth taking a chance on a singular "hit."

My only companion while writing, except for my Bible and computer, was the TV, for background noise. For me, quiet has been a long-time enemy. In the past, quiet would allow my innermost negative thoughts to manifest and, once manifested, become a downward spiral of ruminations that culminate in self-loathing.

You may have noticed that the title of this book is *Shameless* and not *Shame-Free* or *Free from Shame* or *Shame No More*. I've come to realize and understand that shame is a battle that I will most likely fight for the rest of my life. I will always have to fight the temptation to give into shame. Remember that we are delivered from evil, but not temptations. Temptations will be a lifelong battle. However, I know I can give in to shame less and less. I also know that writing this book potentially sets me up for an even broader battle with shame, depending on the reaction it receives.

Before allowing this to be published I had to prepare myself that there will be negative and critical responses that will require me to put into practice the very things you will read about. Ironically, even positive responses can cause me to revert to shame-based thinking because I will be tempted to feel as if I don't deserve anything good, and that at any moment the other shoe may drop.

I am prepared that some well-intended Christians may take me to task. Writing this book is, in some ways, equivalent to being in certain Christian circles where I don't feel the freedom to say that I have a cold. Sometimes an admission like that is met with, "Don't confess that, brother!" or "You're not sick, you're healed!" Now I get where they're coming from, and I believe in the unlimited power of God, but when my nose is running, my ears are clogged, and I have a tissue stuffed into my nostrils, I have a cold. I am not denying that God has the power to heal me or do miracles, but the reality is at this moment I have a cold, and I know that He is aware of it.

Not only is God aware when I have a cold, He may have even allowed it (remember the book of Job?). My view that shame could hound me for the rest of my life may be offensive to some, but I look at it the way Paul dealt with his *"thorn in the flesh"* in 1 Corinthians 12:7–10. Though this thorn could and would harass him, it could not and would not master or control him. Shame will probably harass me every chance it gets, but it will not master or control me. As the Apostle Paul says,

> *"I have the right to do anything," you say—but not everything is beneficial. "I have the right to do anything"—but I will not be mastered by anything.*
> —1 Corinthians 6:12

So some might feel that I am making a negative confession concerning this battle with shame, believing that I am completely healed. And to that I say, "Yes and amen." However, we shouldn't juxtapose or conflate justification and sanctification. One is instantaneous and the other is a process. I believe my spirit is saved by grace through faith in Jesus Christ (Ephesians 2:8) and that in Him I stand blameless before God, all while my soul is being continually restored (2 Corinthians 4:16).

Part of my justification process has included areas and different levels of suffering. The Bible doesn't tell us we will be free of suffering (1 Peter 4:13), but that God's grace is sufficient and that ultimately He works out the good, the bad, and the ugly in our lives for His good purpose (Romans 8:28). My areas and levels of suffering are as unique to me as yours are to you. Not only does God uniquely dispense gifts to us, I believe He also allows us to be uniquely wounded for His purposes. I suffer in areas that others don't and vice versa. And I can unreservedly state that others have suffered at greater and deeper levels than me. To them I offer my prayers.

This book is not for everyone. Some people may read this and scoff that this is much ado about nothing. And to them I say, "Good on you," because if shame is not something you've battled, I am so very, very, and again I say very happy for you.

I believe that shame has at least some influence in almost everyone's life, but some are more affected by it than others. Not only are we uniquely designed and gifted, we are likewise uniquely prone to certain weaknesses and wounding. What may hurt your feelings may not bother another in the least. Some are not as prone to suffer from the effects of shame. Psalm 19 actually provides some insight in this regard.

> *The law of the Lord is perfect, refreshing the soul. The statutes of the Lord are trustworthy, making wise the simple. The precepts of the Lord are right, giving joy to the heart. The commands of the Lord are radiant, giving light to the eyes. The fear of the Lord is pure, enduring forever. The decrees of the Lord are firm, and all of them are righteous. They are more precious than gold, than much pure gold; they are sweeter than honey, than honey from the honeycomb. By them your servant is warned; in keeping them there is great reward. But who can discern their own errors? Forgive my hidden faults. Keep your servant also from willful sins; may they not rule over me. Then I will be blameless, innocent of great transgression. May these words of my mouth and this meditation of my heart be pleasing in your sight, Lord, my Rock and my Redeemer.*
>
> —Psalm 19:7–14

In verses 12–14, there are words whose underlying meaning may help reinforce what I am saying. The words are errors, hidden faults, and willful sins.

Errors are the sins and offenses we commit unknowingly or in ignorance. Willful sins are self-explanatory, but for the sake of having the time to write it out, willful sins are the sins we commit willfully… knowingly… on purpose! It's those hidden faults that make us more or less prone to certain temptations, sensitivities, or offenses. A hidden fault is another way of saying "our specific and personal propensity toward sin." Wouldn't it make sense that if God has designed us down to our minutest physical detail, He would also exert the same power to create us down to our minutest emotional and mental detail?

That's why you can have three children who are made up of your and your spouse's DNA, and yet they are all completely different in their musical, culinary, and fashion tastes. Likewise your children will be completely different in what tempts or entices them.

Similar to the Apostle Paul's thorn in the flesh, shame is something that will probably harass me for the rest of my life. The difference now is that it will not master me, because God's grace is sufficient. For most of my life I was on the losing side of the battle with shame, but by God's more than sufficient grace I'm now experiencing victory upon victory.

For those who read this and can relate, I hope this book provides some healing and relief.

For those who read this and discern that shame is not a strong influence in their life, I hope that they themselves may become enlightened and tenderer toward those who suffer under the thumb of shame. And maybe this book will help them to help others to become shame*less*.

My hopes and prayers are for those who read this and realize they have been battling shame for a lifetime but didn't know its name. If you are the latter or know someone who fits this narrative, I hope and pray that my journey helps to strengthen, comfort, and encourage.

Oh, and by the way, truth be told, I still experience some traditional stage fright or butterflies, but nowhere near what I used to deal with. I could eat a hamburger while walking onstage now… but then I'd need to write a good joke to go with the hamburger.

2.

Now Would Be Nice!

"HELP!" IS WHAT ANY WELL-ADJUSTED PERSON MIGHT YELL IF THEY WERE SWIMMING IN the ocean and realized that the waves had picked up and were pushing them farther from the boat, which they were swimming toward. Not many people would respond with, "Pardon me. If it's not too terribly inconvenient, would you kindly untie that life preserver? No, no, not that one… the blue one… yes, that's the one I prefer. Now, would you kindly toss it to me in an arc-like fashion, so I might retrieve it and thereby preserve my life a little longer and keep me from being swept away?"

There are circumstances in life that require a less-than-refined response, and with all due respect to my cotillion and charm school friends, it's more than appropriate to scream your head off, and even use some salty language if and when you are in distress.

Another scenario that would elicit a less-than-refined request for assistance would be if you were on an airplane and the flight attendant informed you that both the pilot and co-pilot had become incapacitated by food poisoning and you had to go to the cockpit and land the plane. I seriously doubt that you or I would enter the cockpit with much dignity, calmly slide into the pilot's seat, securely place the headset over our ears, and then politely say, "Hello. Yes, if anyone is listening, I'd like to learn the laws of aerodynamics." Most likely you would react like me.

First, assume this is someone's idea of a very sick joke.

Second, inform the flight attendant that she's mistakenly asked the wrong person.

Third, cry like a baby while scrambling to the cockpit, not bothering to sit down, putting on the headset, and screaming, "HELP!" into the microphone.

Situations such as I described require immediate help. No time to make an appointment, stand on ceremony, act with dignity, or use your inside voice. And these are certainly not the type of situations that allow for an "I'll get around to dealing with it someday" approach. No, these are situations that require prompt and immediate attention.

Yet here's the rub. Shame's effect is not always as obvious as a swimmer in crisis or an airplane with an incapacitated pilot. Shame has the ability to be blatantly subtle. It hits like a frying pan but lands like a pillow. It's as if shame were a calculating shapeshifter.

You will notice at times that I use personification when referring to shame. The reason is that as a pastor, after years of meeting with countless individuals and couples, I hold the belief that shame is an entity or spirit. In other words, shame is not only a noun and a verb, but also a force. I will expand upon this idea throughout the book.

Helping people to discover how shame may have affected their lives is like trying to wake up your teenaged children on a school day. Some children wake up immediately to face the day. Other children just need five more minutes. And most families have at least one child who requires a parent to stand on their bed, holding a cup of ice water and threatening to pour it on them if they don't get up *now!* In similar fashion, some people are immediately aware of shame's impact while others need more time to think on it. And of course there are those who seem to refuse to wake up to shame's effect on them.

When dealing with shame, or even depression, sometimes the person on the other end of the headset would rather lecture than listen. Because shame is often equated with certain emotions or feelings, like sadness or unworthiness, some may want to enlighten you about the laws of aerodynamics instead of helping you with the immediate crisis of averting a nosedive into the earth.

The thought here is that when someone becomes the involuntary pilot in an emergency, it's a lot like being overwhelmed with shame. When others try to help, they can inadvertently want to fix the person long-term rather than meeting them where they are in the moment. So if you're in the cockpit and overwhelmed, what you need is for someone to tell you what buttons to push and switches to turn rather than teaching you to appreciate the laws of aerodynamics. After all, you can always talk about the deeper things once you've successfully landed the plane.

I wrote this book in part to help you identify whether or not you carry around within yourself any level of shame. And if so, to help you realize your desire to be free of it, as you would want to be rescued from swirling ocean waves or a pilotless aircraft. Shame nags and tugs at our souls, and we often treat it as something we should just learn to accept and endure as a part of our lives. My encouragement for you is to treat shame like a bad roommate and invite it to move out immediately, telling it, "Don't bother to pack up. I'll send your stuff to you."

Here are some simple scenarios to determine whether shame is nagging at you.

- Someone says to you, "I need to speak to you about something," and your first response is that your back breaks into a sweat and you wonder what you did wrong.
- You have a legitimate need or an opinion about something but don't feel safe to share your need or express your opinion.
- You feel that everyone else in the room is smarter or better than you.
- You feel that other people know things that you should know.
- You believe that you deserve all the bad things that have happened to you.

If any of these scenarios feel familiar, I'd like to throw you a life preserver or help you land the plane, so that you can walk out from under the shroud of trauma and begin a shameless life.

3.

If Only I Were Somebody Else

As I previously stated, there are few vocations that provide a person with more opportunities for immediate rejection than stand-up comedy. Why then, with the high probability of public shame, did I choose comedy for a career? I can't really say that I chose comedy… comedy sort of chose me. Even as I kid, I was a contradiction. Though I feared rejection, I craved approval and would willingly put myself in harm's way to get it.

While most boys my age were watching *Bonanza*, *Gunsmoke*, and *The Man from U.N.C.L.E.*, I had a fascination with comedians like Red Skelton and Bill Cosby and loved comedic duos like Abbott & Costello, Martin & Lewis, and watched every road picture that Bing Crosby and Bob Hope ever made. In grade school, I could get a laugh from other kids by quoting the comedy records I listened to every night. I never revealed my sources; I just reveled in the laughter and acceptance being funny would bring. By the way, it was worth every after-school eraser-cleaning project I had to perform when my teachers didn't find me amusing.

The year I was about to enter junior high school, a new comedian arrived on the scene and was nothing like Red Skelton or Bill Cosby. In 1972, George Carlin's comedy style hit like a tidal wave, appealing to the youth generation. He reinvented his conventional comedian's image of a shorthaired, suit-and-tie-wearing joke-teller to that of a longhaired, bearded comic wearing torn jeans and t-shirts. Unfortunately, I still believed that I and I alone had discovered the gold mine of George Carlin's comedy. Standing at the bus stop for my first ever bus ride to school, I mentally rehearsed every line I had memorized from Carlin's "FM & AM" comedy record that had come out the previous January. As the bus pulled to a stop, the door opened and I stepped aboard prepared to give *my* monologue.

The awkward silence of walking to my seat was peppered with head nods and waves to the kids I knew. Once seated, I sized up my surroundings and soon began regaling my fellow bus-mates with George Carlin's best material. Suddenly my bubble burst when someone chimed in, "Hey, that's George Carlin!" With no backup plan for gaining acceptance and affirmation, my plan for a successful seventh grade year came screeching to a halt.

For the previous three years or so I had been known by my schoolmates as the "funny kid," and by my teachers as "that kid." Now I was in danger of being known as the "chubby pimple-faced kid" by my classmates and the "dumb kid" by my teachers. But as I said earlier, at whatever level I chose comedy, it had already chosen me.

That day after I got home from school, I started writing my own material, juvenile as it was. I was not going to give up on getting the approval I craved through comedy. It became a lifelong obsession. Comedy became my way of masking or hiding the shame that I felt so deeply. Most of my comedy was self-deprecating. My thinking was that if I made fun of my acne, weight, or crooked teeth, I could beat others to the punch.

Throughout the rest of my junior and high school years, I was intent on being funny—and not just funny… the funniest. A crowning achievement was my last year in junior high when I was named "wittiest boy" in the class superlatives. Alas, I was unable to repeat that in my senior year of high school (and I'm getting over that a little more every day).

After high school I enrolled in junior college to major in history, but still with an eye on comedy. My plan was to become like Gabe Kaplan's character in the hit 70s sitcom *Welcome Back, Kotter*. Kaplan plays a history teacher, Gabe Kotter, who returns to the dysfunctional high school where he had himself been a student. Using comedy and a gentle touch, he taught history to a classroom of underachieving misfits known as the Sweat Hogs. I wanted to become a real-life Mr. Kotter, because I already knew what it was like being a real-life Sweat Hog.

I'll spare you the details, but within a few years I was trying out comedy in talent shows, pubs, and finally open mic nights, when a real comedy club came to town. I no longer wanted to teach high school history. I wanted to be the next Robin Williams.

In 1978, a quirky new sitcom hit the airwaves with the lead character being an alien from the planet Ork. A *Happy Days* spinoff called *Mork & Mindy* debuted on ABC on September 14, 1978. I was mesmerized by this new comedian who riffed and vamped with words like a jazz saxophonist does with notes. Like George Carlin before him, Robin Williams changed stand-up comedy.

For the next several years, I got better and better as a comedian and performer. I was fortunate to work with some of the biggest names in comedy, and then, after my conversion to Christ, to tour with some of the top Christian bands and solo artists of the day. During those years, as I got better and better at comedy, I also got better at masking my shame—at least while onstage. Friends who knew me back then will most likely tell you that I am much different now. They might tell you that I am easier to be around, that I am less draining, that I am more honest and more at peace.

I've come to the realization that it's not unusual for people who battle shame to go into the entertainment industry; after all, they've had to be creative, quick-thinking, and able to hide behind a character or play a role. For reasons too numerous for me to fathom, the stage is a great place to work out issues.

An example of this is Pink's song from her second album, *Missundaztood*, released in 2001. The second single from this record was the song "Don't Let Me Get Me." I suggest you search for the lyrics on the web and see if what she writes resonates with you.

I doubt very seriously that one day after reading a stack of teen magazines on her tour bus, Pink decided to write a song about angst from a spectator's point of view. I believe that these lyrics were not a songwriter's creative interpretation of another person's shame, but lyrics born out of Pink's own experience with shameful thinking. Pink puts to rhyme and melody to the internal war within so many people who would rather be anyone but who they actually are. The desire to be somebody else is why people battling shame make good actors. So much of the battle is wishing that we were someone else. In fact, anybody else but us.

You may not be in the entertainment industry, but you may be in a vocation that requires you to be in front of people: a sales manager, customer service representative, teacher, pastor, or whatever. Though you may not be on a stage, you may still be on display while working out some of the same thoughts Pink wrote about. I encourage you again to search out this song on the web. You may be surprised that someone else can put words to what you are internally feeling.

4.

Shame's Debut

IT DIDN'T TAKE LONG FOR SHAME TO MAKE ITS DEBUT IN HISTORY. IN FACT IT APPEARED within the first generation... with the first man and woman.

> *When the woman saw that the fruit of the tree was good for food and pleasing to the eye, and also desirable for gaining wisdom, she took some and ate it. She also gave some to her husband, who was with her, and he ate it. Then the eyes of both of them were opened, and they realized they were naked; so they sewed fig leaves together and made coverings for themselves.*
>
> *Then the man and his wife heard the sound of the Lord God as he was walking in the garden in the cool of the day, and they hid from the Lord God among the trees of the garden. But the Lord God called to the man, "Where are you?"*
>
> *He answered, "I heard you in the garden, and I was afraid because I was naked; so I hid."*
>
> *And he said, "Who told you that you were naked?"*
>
> —Genesis 3:6–11

What is interesting about this passage from the first book of the Bible is the question, *"Who told you that you were naked?"* Apparently, shame appeared without an oral invitation. No one said a word, yet the power of shame appeared and caused the first man and woman to sew fig leaves together to make coverings for their nakedness. According to biblical record, Adam and Eve had no shame—that is, until their eyes were opened as a result of them eating the fruit from the tree of knowledge of good and evil. Sadly, it didn't take long for Adam to fall under shame's control. First he and Eve hid themselves. Then Adam became the first human to pay shame forward.

He answered, "I heard you in the garden, and I was afraid because I was naked; so I hid."

And he said, "Who told you that you were naked? Have you eaten from the tree that I commanded you not to eat from?"

The man said, "The woman you put here with me—she gave me some fruit from the tree, and I ate it."

—Genesis 3:10–12

As a result of Adam's shame, he shames Eve, who is already under shame's influence.

Shame is something that is easily shared.

Shame is the ultimate contact sport, and it likes to collide into anyone and everyone.

Shame lurks and prowls around until it finds its prey. Easy targets are people engaged in a war of words. It doesn't take long before shame attaches itself to words that come out of our own mouths when we are angry, wounded, or just fatigued.

Shame is fairly lazy and doesn't need to exert a lot of energy; it just needs a willing host.

King Solomon understood this and warns, *"Sin is not ended by multiplying words, but the prudent hold their tongues"* (Proverbs 10:19).

Once shame makes contact, it's sticky, kind of like a spider's web or the "amoeba game" that youth groups play. If you've never played it, here is the gist. The game starts with one person designated the amoeba, who runs around seeking to tag the other students in a defined area. Once a student is tagged by the amoeba, they stick to or become one with the first student. On and on the game will continue until everyone in the group becomes assimilated into the amoeba. At first there is a lot of running around, because the amoeba is only one student, but as the amoeba begins to grow, the last remaining students are easily absorbed, because the number of "single cells" have decreased and the amoeba is taking up more and more space. The game ends when everyone is part of the amoeba.

Shame is never satisfied until we and everyone else we know are caught up in its sticky web. Before going any farther, let's uncover and define what shame is.

5.

What Is Shame?

THE WORD SHAME MEANS TO COVER OR TO HIDE. ADAM AND EVE'S RESPONSE AFTER having their eyes opened was to cover and hide their nakedness. Shame has a way of leading people to dark and lonely places. Not only did Adam and Eve cover themselves, they actually hid themselves from God… or at least tried to hide.

Shame's strategy is to entice us into believing that if we cover up and hide, no one else will see or know, similar to a three-year-old playing hide and seek. There they stand in the middle of the living room with their eyes tightly shut, believing they are now invisible to everyone. We chuckle knowingly, as this little one has only fooled him or herself. It is kind of like us thinking that if we shut our eyes to our pain and embarrassments, they become invisible to everyone else.

Paradoxically, shame plays the role of a double agent in our lives. First it coaxes us to cover up, and then once safely hidden it seeks any opportunity to expose and uncover us. Then comes the maddening cycle of hiding, followed by being exposed, then trying once again to hide, only to be uncovered again and again.

A lot of people have given in to shame and live a real-life hide and seek game. They have no intention of being found—or they no longer have the strength or courage to run to the safety of "base."

Like that precious three-year-old, try as we might, we cannot hide from God. We are always in plain view of His loving gaze. Remember that He looks upon us as a loving Father (Luke 15) and not as some hard-hearted taskmaster. Over years of hiding, we become a sort of buried treasure that He longs to dig out from under the rubble of guilt and shame.

> *"Who can hide in secret places so that I cannot see them?" declares the Lord. "Do not I fill heaven and earth?"*
>
> —Jeremiah 23:24

Also, He continues the search.

Or suppose a woman has ten silver coins and loses one. Doesn't she light a lamp, sweep the house and search carefully until she finds it? And when she finds it, she calls her friends and neighbors together and says, "Rejoice with me; I have found my lost coin." In the same way, I tell you, there is rejoicing in the presence of the angels of God over one sinner who repents.

—Luke 15:8–10

Lastly, He is more than capable to provide us safe passage to base.

Surely the arm of the Lord is not too short to save, nor his ear too dull to hear.

—Isaiah 59:1

Shame is crafty, deceitful, and not to be trusted. It not only controls our actions, it invades our psyche to take control of our thoughts and feelings. Here is Webster's definition of shame: "a feeling of guilt, regret, or sadness that you have because you know you have done something wrong… ability to feel guilt, regret, or embarrassment… dishonor or disgrace."[1]

Notice how those words have *feelings* attached to them? I doubt that as you read the definition you imagined butterflies or daisy-covered meadows. Instead, it may have triggered some unpleasant memories or feelings from the past. You may have thought of a specific event or a particular person with whom you associate those feelings.

Not to pile on, but I liken shame to one of those late-night infomercials that always includes the phrase "But wait, there's more!" Shame twists like a proverbial knife in the back and will exaggerate and exacerbate feelings to an unkind end. Continue a bit farther down this dark, dank, and lonely alley of feelings with me to uncover just how deeply shame can affect us. Deep breath… here we go. See these synonyms for shame: remorse, self-reproach, anguish, distress, grief, sorrow, and bloodguilt.

Bloodguilt? Ugh!

Here again, there are feelings attached to these words. So often we are controlled more by our feelings than we are the truth. Even writing these words gives me cause to shudder and hunt down a squeegee for my soul.

---

1 "Shame," *Merriam-Webster.com*. Date of access: January 11, 2016 (http://www.merriam-webster.com/dictionary/Shame).

I'm going to get a hug from my wife before I write further.

Okay, I'm back.

Simply reading the definition, synonyms and words related to shame can quickly put a damper on your mood. Some words have power because of the feelings that are attached to them. If I type out the definition of other nouns like chair, potted plant, or ottoman, you can just keep on reading with little or no emotional response… unless a potted plant bullied you. I digress. But when a noun can evoke emotion from simply reading its meaning, that is one very powerful noun!

Shame not only affects our mind and emotions, it also has the power to affect our bodies. Shame can cause people to experience mild to severe symptoms including, but not limited to, stomachache, headache, trembling, difficulty breathing, slouching, ducking of the head, weeping, a burning sensation in the neck or back, blushing, and wringing of the hands… and that's just to name a few.

Pause for a moment and see if you are experiencing any of these. Oh, I forgot to mention anxiety and panic attacks. You're welcome!

In upcoming chapters, I will go into more detail, using my own personal experiences with shame and how it affected me. I can tell you now that I was completely unaware of these manifestations of shame until my wife pointed them out to me. I hope that as you read these stories in later chapters, they will help you discover whether shame is physically affecting you.

What shame relies on to work most effectively in our lives is personifying its name to cover itself. Stealth is shame's primary mode of operation. Because shame causes a person to hide, it has its very own cloaking device built right in.

Think about it. If you are ashamed or embarrassed about something, do you go around talking about it? Do you post it on Facebook or tweet it to your friends? Heavens no! The last thing you want is to shine a light on or draw attention to anything that is an embarrassment. Yet here comes the irony. Just when you have played right into shame's mode of operation and hidden/covered yourself, shame betrays you by turning off the cloaking device, usually delegating a trusted friend or loved one to throw the switch.

I'll bet you're thinking that there's a story behind that last sentence… and you are correct. But that's in another chapter.

6.

Shame vs. Sorrow

Is THERE SUCH A THING AS GOOD OR HEALTHY SHAME? BY ITS VERY DEFINITION, I DON'T believe so. Is there a good or healthy cancer? Remember that shame causes us to cover up, and that leads to hiding. We need not hide, for Jesus set us free from the kingdom of darkness and into His marvelous light—we are a display of His Glory! It is not a loving God who wags a condemning finger in our face when we've sinned. No. That sense of guilty shame and condemnation comes from the accuser of the brethren, not from God who lavishly loves us.

See what great love the Father has lavished on us, that we should be called children of God! And that is what we are!

—1 John 3:1

In him we have redemption through his blood, the forgiveness of sins, in accordance with the riches of God's grace that he lavished on us. With all wisdom and understanding…

—Ephesians 1:7–8

Jesus unveils the tactics of the devil with what some refer to as Satan's job description:

The thief comes only to steal and kill and destroy; I have come that they may have life, and have it to the full.

—John 10:10

The effects of shame in a person's life often reflect these three tactics

1. Shame *steals* our true identity. We are robbed of claiming our birthright, of being fearfully and wonderfully made in the image of a loving God. However, God's Word says that we not only have a birthright, we also receive an inheritance.

Furthermore, because we are united with Christ, we have received an inheritance from God, for he chose us in advance, and he makes everything work out according to his plan.

—Ephesians 1:11, NLT

2. Shame *kills* any hope we have for the plans and future that God has for us. We can no longer dream or believe that we have a purpose for being here. But Jeremiah shares this piece of really good news:

"For I know the plans I have for you," declares the Lord, "plans to prosper you and not to harm you, plans to give you hope *and a* future.*"*

—Jeremiah 29:11–13 (emphasis added)

3. Shame *destroys* whatever good happens in our lives. It makes us believe we don't deserve anything good or that this good is only here until the other shoe drops. But wait, there's more from God's Word, written by none other than Jesus' younger brother:

Every good and perfect gift is from above, coming down from the Father of the heavenly lights, who does not change like shifting shadows.

—James 1:17

Shame's mantra is "would've, should've, and could've." Shame doesn't allow a person to be free of the past, to live in the moment, or hope for the future. In J.R.R. Tolkien's *The Lord of the Rings* trilogy, Frodo gets tangled in a giant spider's web. Like the giant spider Shelob, shame also spins a sticky web, string by string, by string by sticky string. Once trapped, we become emotionally immobilized by its suffocating power.

On the other hand, sorrow allows us to confess openly and confront our wrongs, mistakes, and sins. Sorrow creates a sense of grief, sadness, regret, heartache, or distress. The distinction between shame and sorrow is this: healthy sorrow doesn't deny or cover up our feelings for wrongs we committed; it compels us to restore or to make things right.

Paul does a great job explaining healthy sorrow in his second letter written to the church at Corinth. In a previous letter he dealt with some issues that needed to be openly addressed, and he did so without shaming a particular person or group of people. What his letter ultimately produced was a healthy sorrow that led to distress. Distress is what you feel when you find yourself in a situation that you really want out of.

Let me give you an illustration that shows how healthy sorrow leads to distress, and distress leads to action.

One day on a beach vacation, you paddle out too far in a little rubber raft that has just sprung a leak in shark-infested waters. No matter how good or bad your day was going, now that great whites surround you with dinner on their minds, you've quickly moved beyond sorrow that you paddled out too far. You're way past regretting that you didn't check the seaworthiness of your raft. You are in full-on distress! Every mistake or poor decision that led up to this situation disappears into overwhelming angst. And all you want is to get out!

That's what healthy sorrow does. It moves us beyond stagnation of thought and ruminating on our poor decisions. It compels us to action: to repair and get out of the situation we created or allowed others to create. Shame would rather just feed you to the sharks. Shame blames you for everything gone wrong in the situation and makes you feel like you deserve to be eaten alive.

Here is Paul's follow-up concerning the correction and rebuke from a previous letter:

Even if I caused you sorrow by my letter, I do not regret it. Though I did regret it—I see that my letter hurt you, but only for a little while—yet now I am happy, not because you were made sorry, but because your sorrow led you to repentance. For you became sorrowful as God intended and so were not harmed in any way by us. Godly sorrow brings repentance that leads to salvation and leaves no regret, but worldly sorrow brings death. See what this godly sorrow has produced in you: what earnestness, what eagerness to clear yourselves, what indignation, what alarm, what longing, what concern, what readiness to see justice done. At every point you have proved yourselves to be innocent in this matter.

—2 Corinthians 7:8–11

Notice that Paul was torn about the letter that caused them sorrow, yet his love for them was not compromised, because he brought correction. On the contrary, his love for them compelled his actions.

Correction in and of itself *should not* produce shame in a person. We are to speak the truth in love, instruct with great patience, and gently restore others. Unfortunately, shame is produced when none of these measures of bringing correction is used. The biblical process of correction or rebuke is done in a way that never harms a person, though it may hurt a little while. I wonder if Paul learned this from his dear friend and traveling companion, Dr. Luke?

Though written long after Paul and Luke's mission trips, the Hippocratic Oath is a wonderful reflection of Paul's dealing with the Corinthians. In the oath is the phrase: "I will prescribe regimens for the good of my patients according to my ability and my judgment and never do harm to anyone," which has become the popularized phrase: "Do no harm."

The oath says nothing about *not hurting* anyone. If that were the case, no doctor would ever reset a broken bone, give a lifesaving injection, or make an incision, all of which hurt. A physician may indeed have to hurt us to save us from harm. And like a good physician, Paul hurt the Corinthians in the short-term in order to keep them from long-term harm.

Sometimes shame is exported by unloving or anger-inspired correction. When we bring correction or rebuke, we need to do so in a manner consistent with scripture. Paul encourages a young pastor named Timothy to *"[p]reach the word; be prepared in season and out of season; correct, rebuke and encourage—with great patience and careful instruction"* (2 Timothy 4:2).

Here are a few other scriptures concerning shameless correction:

Instead, speaking the truth in love, we will grow to become in every respect the mature body of him who is the head, that is, Christ.
—Ephesians 4:15

Brothers and sisters, if someone is caught in a sin, you who live by the Spirit should restore that person gently. But watch yourselves, or you also may be tempted. Carry each other's burdens, and in this way you will fulfill the law of Christ.
—Galatians 6:1–2

And for me, these verses sum up the spirit in which we should treat others when bringing correction. On the night He was betrayed, and knowing full well what was about to happen to Him, Jesus taught and modeled one last lesson for His disciples.

Now that I, your Lord and Teacher, have washed your feet, you also should wash one another's feet. I have set you an example that you should do as I have done for you.

—John 13:14–15

Paul did his best to wash the feet of those he was correcting. He commends the leaders and members of the Corinthian church for dealing with issues on which he confronted them. His correction was well-received, as they didn't blame circumstance, each other, or even Paul. They took an open and honest view of the situation, and instead of covering it up, they had a healthy response to their own sins and the sins of others. They didn't retreat... they took action.

Battling shame is not passive. It requires effort to resist the urge to sit idly by and allow self-pity to metastasize into self-hatred. Unless we engage mentally, emotionally, and spiritually, it will be like fighting with our hands tied behind our backs.

We need to plug the leak in our raft, find the strength to paddle back to shore, and yes, even holler, "Shark!" When we are in distress, we don't concern ourselves with appearance. We don't care how silly or foolish we look; we just want help. With distress comes a surge of adrenalin and endorphins that have no intention of feeding the sharks.

Have you ever felt paralyzed by your thoughts? Do you often feel that everything is your fault or feel like you deserve all the bad things that come your way? Well then, you are probably battling shame. These thoughts are influenced by shame and adversely affect your life. Then it's time to take action. Read the following verse out loud.

Therefore, there is now no condemnation for those who are in Christ Jesus, because through Christ Jesus the law of the Spirit who gives life has set you free from the law of sin and death.

—Romans 8:1–3

It's been my experience that condemnation is shame's little buddy. Condemnation means "the expression of very strong disapproval, criticism, denunciation and vilification" and "the action of condemning someone [even ourselves] to punishment and sentencing."[2] Condemnation provides no grace, no hope, and only negative judgments. Now read this verse out loud.

> *Do not conform to the pattern of this world, but be transformed by the renewing of your mind. Then you will be able to test and approve what God's will is—his good, pleasing and perfect will.*
>
> —Romans 12:2

Perhaps you battle shame because of how you were corrected by a parent, teacher, coach, or even pastor. Proper correction brings a sorrow that strengthens us to make things right, encourages us to rid ourselves of guilt, and comforts us with hope. If we were not corrected or rebuked properly, we may develop a pattern of thinking that produces a taste for shame. This acquired taste or mindset doesn't take long to develop, but it can take a lifetime to undo.

Much of how we see the world and view ourselves develops in childhood. In those formative years, we think like a child, so sometimes what we thought about a situation is completely incorrect. A thought pattern of shame can be so ingrained in us that we don't even realize it.

For example, a child might believe that Mommy hates him because she is angry that there is spilled milk on the floor. Very few, if any, four-year-olds think to themselves, *Gee, Mommy sure is upset about that milk on the floor because hardwoods are so hard to clean. I am certain that she is not angry with me; after all, I didn't intend to spill the milk. I'll just wait until she stops yelling, and we'll talk about her feelings.* Four-year-old children think like four-year-old children. So when Mommy is upset about the spilled milk, most four-year-olds think Mommy is upset at them.

The Apostle Paul writes that when he was a child, he thought and acted like a child, but when he became a man, he put childish thinking behind him. That is what Romans 12:2 is all about. As children, we may have developed a pattern of thinking that comes from the world (condemnation) and not from God (grace). We must resist conforming to the thought pattern that we are always the problem and renew our thought pattern to reach out for God's mercy and grace.

There is a wonderful verse in Paul's second letter to the church at Corinth that would be a very helpful in renewing our minds.

---

2 *Webster's Collegiate Dictionary*, Third Edition of the Merriam Series, "Condemnation" (Springfield, MA: G. & C. Merriam Co., 1928).

We demolish arguments and every pretension that sets itself up against the knowledge of God, and we take captive every thought to make it obedient to Christ.
—2 Corinthians 10:5

Shame argues against the truth of God's grace. Shame's opinion of us is that we'll never measure up and that we're worthless. So in order to transform our minds, we need to lean on the knowledge of God and place our negative thoughts about ourselves into the big, strong, nail-scarred hands of Jesus to hold those thoughts captive so that they do not take us captive. I remember reading somewhere that Jesus has *"set the oppressed free"* (Luke 4:18).

7.

The Whiteboard

WHENEVER WE HAVE BEEN WRONGED OR WOUNDED AND WE PURPOSE IN OUR HEART, soul, and mind to move on and forgive, why is it so stinking hard? I mean, we really do want to move on and forgive them, don't we?

Yes, of course we do! But maybe not yes... just yet.

Forgiveness is a choice, a decision, and a process. I can't tell you how many times I really thought I had forgiven someone (or even myself) and the next thing you know I'm grinding my teeth just thinking about that someone else or that so-and-so. What to do, what to do? Maybe this illustration will help you like it helped me.

Picture a dry erase board. Have you noticed that the first few times you use it, it erases pretty well? But then after a while, even though you erased what was written, you can still see a faded version of the words. The more you write and erase, write and erase, the more dingy the board becomes. Now let's put that dry erase board in a teacher's classroom. Even though the teacher erased the board from what was written in the previous class, when you enter the classroom you can still make out what was previously written. In order to get the board really clean, you have to do two things.

First, don't leave the writing on the board for too long, for the longer the words stay on the whiteboard, the harder it is to clean them off.

Second, at some point you will have to do more than just use the eraser. You will need a cleaning solution that is specifically designed to clean the board completely.

Hurtful spoken words that linger in our hearts are hard to get rid of. The scripture says that *"an undeserved curse does not come to rest [upon us]"* (Proverbs 26:2). Yet we often will take hold of, and even nurture, hurtful words directed toward us. How do I know this? You are looking at the champ! I've had a history of taking flippant, offhanded comments directed at me and turning them into full-on unlawful, mean-spirited self-prosecutions. Once shame was introduced into my life, I, more than any other person or circumstance, was the chief architect of the shame shrine being erected in my psyche.

Instead of quickly erasing the words, I allowed them to soak into the whiteboard of my heart, so that by the time I decided to erase them, there remained a word residue. And once there is some word residue, it's very easy to acquire more and more. Trust me on this: when we harbor or hold on to ill feelings, it doesn't take long for other people to make out what was previously written on the whiteboard of our hearts.

This was my pattern. Sure, I was teased, mocked, and made fun of, but I gave the words and actions more power than they really had. I took hold of them, I dwelled on them, and I, and I alone, was responsible for the growing power that shame had in my life. I don't blame anyone else for how strong shame became, and I don't even blame myself. I did, however, need to recognize and take responsibility for its growth and malignancy so that I could forgive and move forward.

In order to truly forgive, I realized that within myself there was no chance of forgiving others until I was first forgiven. I required a solution specific to cleaning my own heart. The innocent, shed blood of Jesus Christ was that cleaning solution. Jesus, who was without sin, took upon Himself my sin (and the penalty for my sin) so that in Him I could experience a new life. Upon the cross Jesus suffered, bled, and died to cleanse me of all unrighteousness. Without the blood of Jesus, the words written on the whiteboard of my heart could never be fully erased. I don't have that kind of power; I only had an eraser and some elbow grease. No amount of self-effort or elbow grease can clean the human heart. Only Jesus has that kind of cleaning power.

Ask the Lord to give you the strength you need in this moment to forgive. Don't think about tomorrow's needed strength; just get through this moment so that you can get through the next chapter.

8.

Exposing Shame without Paying It Forward

FORGIVENESS HAS ALLOWED ME TO BECOME GRATEFUL FOR DIFFICULT EVENTS AND situations in my life that were painful at one time. By forgiving others (and myself), I have gained life lessons rather than accumulated a collection of bad memories. To be helpful, a level of self-disclosure is required. With that in mind, I want to be careful not to pay forward any shame as I recall past events. People whom I love and who love me, both living and passed, will be mentioned from time to time, but with fondness and a grateful heart.

I hope this will help empower you to bravely face your own history—how shame has affected and influenced the way you feel and act.

Shame entered my life at an early age, so keep in mind that like the Apostle Paul, I thought like a child back then. I believe it was unintentional on the part of others for me to feel shame, but shame couldn't care less whether it's intentional or not. Shame will kick down doors as readily as it covertly, and seemingly innocently, rings the doorbell. Shame took shape and form in my life by attaching more to others' words and actions than those people may have ever intended.

"I've had nothing but pure hell for ten years!" my mother uttered to no one in particular. She was just angry. Though Mom didn't talk about it much, I've since come to realize that she endured a difficult childhood. I remember my grandmother being very critical and impatient with Mom. The only happy memory she ever shared was of her father, and he passed away when she was young.

When I was an infant, our father decided that he loved someone else, so our mother became a single parent of three children. As Mom struggled on her own to provide for my older sister, brother, and me, her ability to cope started to come from a wine bottle. Sadly, over the next few years, Mom's source of comfort became an addiction to alcohol.

When Mom drank, my siblings and I got out of sight. Our mother was a lovely, witty, strong, highly intelligent, and well-educated woman. And when she was not drinking, she was extremely charming, funny, and engaging. Years of drinking changed all that. When I look at old photos of her before she started drinking, it's like looking at a completely different person. Mom became less charming, less engaging, and angrier. And anger is not a good mixer with alcohol.

But being a young child, I knew and understood none of what I just wrote. All I knew back then was that Mom was mad and I just assumed she was mad at me. When Mom would utter, "I've had nothing but pure hell for eleven years," I knew that I was eleven, Mom was not happy, and I believed it was because of me.

Making it even more difficult, this was at a time when divorce was not as prevalent, or even acceptable, as it is today. It wasn't until I was in middle school that I met another kid whose parents were divorced.

As kids, we heard little about Mom's childhood, about our dad, or about how hurtful the divorce process was. Mom didn't talk about it to us, and I'm pretty sure she didn't talk about it much to anybody else. This was not uncommon in that era; people just got on with life and learned an unhealthy way of dealing with it: she stuffed it.

Mom was a popular and much beloved teacher at my high school, and she developed a knack that allowed her to stuff and suppress her feelings during the day. By the way, not to brag or anything, but my mom was an *amazing* teacher. In the classroom, Mom was marvelous. She was funny, engaging, and very entertaining. She was also very strong and would not suffer fools in her classroom. She set the bar high and her students went to great lengths not to disappoint her.

However, when Mom came home from school, she would open a bottle of "coping," and what she had suppressed during the day would soon leak out at night. Have you ever heard the expression "Hurt suppressed will become anger expressed"? That was my mom. She tried so hard to bury the stress, hurt, and shame she felt. But no one—not even my super strong, highly intelligent, and well-educated mother—can bury hurt and shame for long.

Please understand that my mother never, ever blamed me for my father's departure. She never, ever wanted to hurt or discourage me. However, I always *felt* that it was my fault. *Felt* is the crucial word. I *felt* that it was my fault because Mom's timeline of pure hell always coincided with my age. When she'd say, "I've had twelve years of hell," you guessed it... I was twelve years old. This oft-repeated phrase burnished in me a feeling which became a belief system. Consequently, being ashamed of what I mistakenly believed, I never, not even once, shared with anyone my feelings or belief that I was the cause of my father's leaving until many, many years later.

9.

What's in a Name?

ANOTHER EARLY EXPERIENCE THAT PLAYED A ROLE IN DEVELOPING MY BATTLE WITH shame had to do with a deep-rooted belief that I was stupid. When I would not quickly grasp something in school, I would default to this belief and not ask my teachers any questions, because I assumed I was the only stupid kid in the class.

Though shame operates in many forms, it does most of its damage through the power of words. In the book of Proverbs, King Solomon explains the power of words:

> *The tongue has the power of life and death, and those who love it will eat its fruit.*
> —Proverbs 18:21

James the brother of Jesus is a little less poetic in his assessment:

> *The tongue also is a fire, a world of evil among the parts of the body. It corrupts the whole body, sets the whole course of one's life on fire, and is itself set on fire by hell.*
> —James 3:6

We can shame with a rolling of our eyes, a wink, a sigh, a dismissive tsk, or gazing skyward in annoyance. These tend to have a momentary shaming effect on others. Words, however, linger for days, weeks, and even years.

Usually a nickname is something bestowed upon someone that denotes endearment. Sweet pea, honeybun, sugar, squirt, angel, etc. are nicknames that we give our children. Sometimes nicknames are bestowed because of something embarrassing. Stink Butt, Tooter, and Poop Face are probably not nicknames you would choose for yourself. And the worst part of unwanted nicknames? They stick!

When I was ten years old, ADHD had not yet been diagnosed, or if it was, they never told me. I had the attention span of a cocker spaniel puppy, and if I thought it, I said it. Many times I was encouraged to think before I spoke; however, that was not in my repertoire of gifts and talents at the time.

I tried not talking at all, but sooner or later what I held back for those few minutes of silence would come pouring out. So I had a few nicknames given to me by family members, like Motor-Mouth, Chatty Cathy, and Mighty-Mouth. None of those stuck. However, one nickname did stick around for a while, and it was the last one I would have ever chosen: Dumb Steve.

My sister had a friend whom my family and I all loved. I always admired and looked up to him, for he was one of the funniest people I've ever known. He was also very intelligent, generous, and wouldn't intentionally hurt anyone... not even the proverbial fly.

The summer before my seventh year of school, my sister, her friend, my brother, and I were all in our front yard throwing a Frisbee® around, when I tried to enter into the conversation my sister was having with her friend. I don't recall what I said, but I can almost guarantee it was something I made up just to sound like I knew what I was talking about. But boy do I remember what her friend said: "Okay, Dumb Steve, just throw the Frisbee." Dumb Steve landed on me like a branding iron.

No one meant for the name to last or to affect me. It was said in a moment and intended to be humorous. I know from the bottom of my pancreas that neither my sister's friend nor my siblings intended to hurt me that day or in the future, but shame intended to brand the belief that I was dumb and stupid into my soul.

Shame waits for any opportunity to pounce on words said by another. From that day and for many years to come, Dumb Steve hung around my neck like a noose. Even after people stopped calling me that! No one had to say it anymore, because I came to believe it. Shame attached itself to yet another part of my psyche and soul. Now my belief system said that I not only caused my mother's hell, I was stupid, too!

Later that same year, my mother was upset about a school rezoning, which meant that instead of being able to walk to school, I would be bussed more than fifteen miles away from our neighborhood. (This was the same bus ride where I trotted out my stolen comedy routine.) She and other parents protested this rezoning by keeping their children out of school the first two weeks. So while everyone else in my math class was learning how to use a compass to measure angles, I stayed at my aunt and uncle's house.

My first day at school was the day my math class took the compass test. My teacher, who wasn't thrilled with the students who were held out for the first two weeks, handed me a compass to "borrow" because on the first day of school my classmates received a list of items we needed to purchase, and of course I never got the list that included the compass.

I took my seat and had no clue how to use the compass. I peeked around to see what the other kids were doing, but never really got the clue that the little hole in the compass played a major role in answering the questions. Needless to say, I failed the test. In fact, I was the only kid who failed. And I was the only one who got all the answers wrong.

I remember that day like it was today—that day was also the first time I ever sweated through my clothing. Not only was I the new kid in school, now more than ever I felt like Dumb Steve. I was now the dumb kid in school… with sweaty armpits! This pattern of feeling dumb at school, especially in math, followed me for the next several years.

I can still wake up in a cold sweat thinking about ninth grade algebra. The kindest way to say this is that my teacher may have missed her calling as a prison guard or a villain in a classic fairy tale. She may very well have even been the inspiration behind the story of Hansel and Gretel. It would not surprise me in the least if she had a gingerbread house and ate little children, particularly boys.

She was sharp-tongued, quick-witted, sarcastic, and utilized shame like an artist might use paint or clay. I am fairly confident that she learned her shaming craft from someone else from her own life experiences. In her defense, she did have to teach a bunch of middle school kids the concepts and principles of complicated mathematics all day long. The problem was that algebra was my second to last class of the day, and my teacher and I were both schooled-out by then.

By the time fifth period rolled around, what my algebra teacher did was scroll through the equations she had previously written on the overhead projector (remember those?) four times earlier that day. She was less than enthusiastic—and did I mention she gave off the vibe that she wasn't a big fan of boys?

Let's do a little math word problem right now.

My mother felt abandoned by the men in her life + I felt like it was my fault that my dad left + my nickname is Dumb Steve + It took a lot longer for me to figure out that compass thing than the other kids + I have undiagnosed ADHD + the "green sister" incident = don't ask any questions because you're just too dumb to do math.

Oh wait… you don't know about the "green sister" incident, do you?

My Sister is Green (and the Sky is Purple)

NOT TO BEAT A DEAD HORSE, BUT REMEMBER THAT SHAME IS CRAFTY AND WILL USE moments in our lives to incorporate what appears to be a strategy. It might help to understand why Dumb Steve landed so well upon me if you know that there was already a foundation laid when I was in the second grade.

My teacher stood over me while I colored and worked on what was sure to be a masterpiece. She looked puzzled and then asked, "Stephen, who is that?" She was pointing at what anyone else could tell was a rendering of my sister.

"That's my big sister!" I said with pride.

"Do you not like her?"

"I love my sister; she's my best friend!"

"Then why did you color her green?"

"Because she *is* green!"

I wish I had said that last sentence a bit softer, because my entire class was now looking at me. My teacher, for whatever reason, thought I was being a smart aleck. She was neither amused nor interested in my green sister and changed the subject.

"And why did you color the sky purple?" she asked with a tinge of frustration in her voice.

"It's not purple, it's blue!" I said with my own tinge of frustration.

My teacher must have been part ninja, because in a blink of an eye I was out of my seat and tippy-toeing down the aisle of desks as she dragged me by my upper arm to the door. I remember hearing gasps mixed with giggles as I exited the classroom in midair, being swung into the hallway.

She leaned over and nearly touched my nose with hers. "Listen here, little mister," she hissed. "I do not suffer smart alecks in my classroom. Now you stop being a fool, and tell me why you colored your sister green and the sky purple!"

I had never heard "suffer" used in a sentence like that before, and I really can't blame her for being frustrated. I now understand that working with a lot of children sometimes can get a little irritating, especially if you believe a child is deliberately being obstinate. But I can assure you, if the child were shaking as hard as I was and with eyes wide as saucers, I would realize that child was being serious. Unfortunately, I wasn't the one working with children that day.

Once again I found myself tippy-toeing as my teacher reapplied her bear-trap grip on my upper arm. We "walked" together that way straight to the principal's office, where you and I both know an electric paddle resides for bad little boys and girls. She swung me into the office like she had swung me out of the classroom, and into a chair.

"I need to speak to the principal!" she said to the nice lady at the front counter.

That lady was the one to whom we brought our notes from home when we were tardy or needed to leave early for doctor appointments and such. She and I had a good thing going, until now. Surprisingly, she smiled at me, as if she understood how frightened and confused I was.

"He's not here at the moment. Can I help you?" the very nice lady at the counter said.

"I have to get back to my classroom," said my teacher. "You have him call me, as soon as he gets back, to deal with this little monster."

As scared as I was, all I could see in my mind's eye when she said "monster" was Frankenstein. Apparently this thought produced a smile that my teacher interpreted as a smirk.

That took her to a new level of rage, and she shook me by both arms and yelled, "You are in for it, little mister! You are going to stop saying that people are green!"

Then she stormed out of the office, and I burst into tears.

"It's okay, Stephen," said the kind lady from behind the front counter. She put her arms around me and almost rocked me like we were in a rocking chair. "You're a good boy, and it's going to be okay."

Now you may be wondering how I can recall this so well. Me too! Sometimes I can't remember what I ate for lunch, or if I even ate at all. I forget appointments, names, phone numbers, and will even forget what my wife asked me to get for her from the kitchen ten seconds earlier. Yet for some reason I can recall in vivid detail moments of extreme joy and dread. I can remember every single detail of my children's births. I remember the names of the nurses, what I was wearing, and even what I ate those days. I remember it like watching a movie, and I love it. I also can recall in vivid detail moments that I wish I could forget. Our brains have a capacity that few humans take advantage of, but this is more than brain usage. These types of moments are seared into our souls as much as our memories.

Now let's go back to the principal's office.

Have you ever cried so hard that you have aftershocks? It's difficult to catch your breath and you make these awful guttural sounds as you try to settle down. Well, that was where I was, trying as hard as I could to stop crying—the more I tried, the greater the aftershocks. The very kind lady from behind the counter (most likely an angel sent from heaven) just sat there and held me until and eventually the principal walked in. I had never talked to him or been in his office before, but he addressed me by name.

"Well, hello, Stephen. What brings you here today?" he said gently.

Obviously he had not seen my teacher or he would have already fired up the electric paddle. I opened my mouth, and all that came out were a new round of aftershocks. The nice lady behind the counter, who most likely has a mansion in heaven, took the principal aside and whispered to him. He occasionally looked back at me and smiled.

"Stephen, come with me to my office," he said in a way that felt like an invitation rather than a command. "Would like something to drink?"

Looking back on this, it was like being asked what you'd like for your last meal before facing death, but I didn't know about things like that yet, so I asked for some water. To my utter amazement he opened a little glass bottle of Coca-Cola and handed it to me.

"Here you go, son. Now, what's this visit all about?"

(By the way, I can recall every time a man called me "son," but that's another chapter and don't skip ahead.)

As best I could, I retold the story about my green sister and the blue sky that my teacher had said was purple. All he did was nod and say "Uh-huh" every now and then.

When I finished, he had more questions for me.

"Stephen, what color is my tie?" He held it up away from his shirt so I could see it better.

"It's blue," I replied, to which he responded with "Hmm."

"Okay then, what color is this book?" he asked, holding up a Dr. Seuss book.

"It's red," I said, hoping I had answered correctly, because there were a lot of colors on the cover.

Again all he said was "Hmm."

He thought for a moment, looked at his tie, then the book. Then he called to his secretary: "Get me Barbara Geyer on the phone. She's a teacher at the high school."

All I could think was, *Oh my God, I am so going to get it!*

Immediately I began crying, and the principal came around from behind his desk and knelt down next to the chair in which I was sitting.

"Stephen... Stephen... it's okay, it's okay," he said reassuringly. "You are not in trouble. I just need to ask your mom something."

While the new aftershocks were ebbing away, he spoke to my mom on the phone.

All I heard was his side of the conversation. It went like this: "Hi Barbara, it's Gene. How are you today? Good, good. I'm fine, thanks for asking. The reason I'm calling is that I have Stephen here in my office... no, no, he's not hurt, and no, he's not in any trouble. We've just been talking, and I wanted to ask you something... "

At that, he turned his swivel chair away from me and asked a question that I couldn't hear.

"Ah, okay," he said, turning his chair back, again facing me. "That's what I thought. We'll talk some more, and I'll call you later."

He hung up the phone, then paused and smiled at me before getting up from his desk and walking over to a large bookcase. He hummed as he selected two books that were thick, but small like a postcard. He sat down in the chair next to me and opened one of the books.

"Stephen, do you see the number 7?" he asked, showing me a picture of a bunch of dots and no number 7 on it.

"No, sir," I answered.

"Hmm" was all he said as he turned to the next page. "Do you see the capital letter A?" He showed me another weird picture of dots.

"No, sir," I replied, this time feeling like I was giving the wrong answer.

"Hmm," he said, opening the other little book. "Do you see a star?"

All I could see were a bunch of dots, but I strained as hard as I could and searched for a star for several seconds.

He chuckled. "It's okay if you don't see it, Stephen, and straining isn't going to help. How about now... do you see the star now?"

He made the sign of a star on the page.

"Sort of, I guess so," I replied, actually catching glimpses of a star shape as he continued retracing his finger over the star.

"How about now?" he asked, no longer tracing the star with his finger.

"No, sir," I said. "It's okay, Stephen. The reason you can't see them is because you're colorblind."

So often what makes us different or unique is met with anything but acceptance and celebration. I have friends who have visible birthmarks and grew up with people saying things like "What the heck is that? You have something on your face. I'd see a doctor about that. That's so weird looking!" I wish I had the time to share with you some stories from parents of children with special needs, but that's a whole other book. Other than having a gap between my two front teeth, I sort of blended in with most other kids. I wasn't unusually tall, short, slim, or heavy; I was just sort of average on the outside.

Oh great, just great, my uniqueness had to do with being colorblind.

When I say colorblind, I don't mean that I only see in black and white. I see colors, but not necessarily like most people see them. I get blue and purple mixed up a lot. Green and yellow are an adventure. Red and green sometimes cook my noodle. I see colors, but don't always see them correctly. Apparently that's not a good thing when you're supposed to be coloring a picture of your family to be put on the classroom bulletin board for the school's upcoming open house.

Even to this day, my wife has to pick out my outfits, so they will match at some level. Maybe one day I'll share the story of when I was trying to buy some running shoes, and my then-four-year-old son had to match them for me.

The reason I colored my sister green is because she has an olive complexion—and I see that as a vivid green. And the reason I colored the sky purple is because I'm colorblind.

My principal walked me back to my classroom and had me stand in the hallway while he went in to the classroom to ask my teacher to meet us out in the hallway. He explained to her what the issue was and assured her that I wasn't sassing her or being obstinate. He asked if she had any questions, to which she replied "No," and then I followed her back into the classroom.

To this day, I wish I could have talked to her later in life to ask her about that day. Sadly, she passed away not many years after this incident. The reason I have questions is because of what happened next. She was apparently still seething about what had happened and decided to take out her frustrations on me in front of my classmates.

Like our family system, school experiences can also be a breeding ground for shame. And like family, it can come from adults and kids alike. I believe that there has never been a teacher who went to college, earned a teaching degree, and received a teaching certificate who ever said, "My desire is to shame as many students as I can before I die!" No teacher I have ever met, anyway, would say that. But yet, it happens more often than anyone would care to admit. I also don't believe that my second grade teacher set out to shame me that day. It just happened that way.

After returning to my desk, my teacher held up the "masterpiece" with my green sister and purple sky and said to the class, "Can anyone tell me what color the sky is in this picture?"

"Purple!" they all shouted.

"That's right, it is purple, but Stephen thinks it's blue!" she said sarcastically. "And this is his sister, who he says is green!"

I don't recall seeing much for the next few moments, as I had put my head down on my arms on my desk, but I heard her say, "Stephen is colorblind. Now, isn't that interesting?" she said with a mocking lilt at the end of her question. She then told me to look up at her, and when I did she pointed to a cabinet and said, "Stephen, what color is that?"

For the next minute or so, she pointed at various items in the classroom, asking me what color they were. Some I guessed correctly and some were a total miss. Some of my classmates were giggling, but most seemed to be looking at me as if they felt sorry for me. Why she did that, I will never know. I can only suppose that someone somewhere had probably shamed her, and with that thought in mind, I am compelled to extend grace and forgiveness to her.

You may have a similar story. My own son does. His story happened when he was in the fourth grade. If you do have similar story or event, I want to share another story, about another teacher… another *math* teacher. But this next story is much different from the one you just read.

11

Undoing Shame

It is ironic that when I was in high school, a teacher—more specifically, a math teacher—lifted some shame off me. For most of my school years, I was an average student and often had the words "Is capable of doing much better work" written on my report cards. As a kid battling shame, I interpreted that sentence as "Do better!" Now as an adult, I've learned to focus on "Is capable." Reading those words today, I take them as encouragement that I have the potential to do well. When I was a kid, however, I interpreted those words to mean "You're a failure."

I thank God that I can now read those words as a man, and not a shame-filled little boy. And thank God for Mrs. Van Hooydonk.

Man, this test is a breeze, I thought to myself as I wrote the answers to each question while making sure that I "showed my work" in the margins. I was in the tenth grade, sitting in a remedial math class with all the other "dumb" kids, taking a test on what we had been learning all week. I walked up to my teacher's desk, laid my paper down, and went back to my seat. When I noticed everyone else was still working on the test, my back broke out in a sweat, and my first thought was, *I must have answered every question wrong, because they're all still working on the problems.*

I was looking around at my classmates when my teacher called me up to her desk.

Oh no, I must have really blown it.

When I got to her desk, she leaned forward and quietly asked, "Stephen, what are you doing in my class?"

I assumed that she saw me looking around and thought that I was cheating.

"Oh, I turned in my test," I said nervously, pointing at the paper she was currently holding. "I was just looking around the room."

She smiled and told me to come around the desk and stand next to her.

Holding my test where I could see it, she said, "I'm not asking about what you were just doing, I'm asking why you were assigned to remedial math class?"

Before I even had to think, I knew the answer. "Because I'm stupid," I replied matter-of-factly.

I was stunned when her eyes welled with tears. "Stephen, you are not stupid! You are very smart."

That's when my eyes welled up. That was the first time I can recall someone ever saying that I was smart, as an affirmation. I'd been told many times before that I was smart, but always as a pejorative and followed by "aleck."

"Stephen, look at your grade." She pointed to the capital letter A with a plus sign next to it. Apparently I'd gotten the extra credit question right, too. "Why are you in my class?" she asked again.

"I don't understand algebra," I said, looking at the floor.

What she asked next made me feel like she knew about something that I had never told anyone. "Stephen, is it that you don't understand algebra or is it that you've never been taught algebra?"

I'd never had the thought—or if I did, I'd never told anyone—that the reason I didn't understand algebra was because I was never *taught* algebra. I just assumed that everyone else in middle school grasped the concepts, and I was too dumb to get it.

For the next few minutes, Mrs. Van Hooydonk taught me some basic rules of algebra. She spoke in a way that I understood and kept saying, "You'll get this... you'll get this." Then she wrote down a problem, handed me her pencil, and smiled. "Solve this."

As I began solving the problem, and made sure to show my work in the margins, I felt as if a coat of iron were being lifted off me.

Now it's not cool to cry in high school (especially while doing math), but as I finished solving the problem and handed back her pencil, I was fighting back tears. She looked over my work, then stood up from her chair, hugged me, and exuberantly declared, "Yes!"

(Okay... I cried, so what!)

In a matter of a few minutes, Mrs. Van Hooydonk had lifted off layers of shame that had built up for many years. I wish that I didn't have to use parentheses in the previous sentence. Shame lost its grip on me in those few moments, and I genuinely experienced a sense of freedom, but because of long-held inner beliefs, a family system that included shame, and no one to reaffirm what Mrs. Van Hooydonk said, it wasn't long before the iron coat was back.

I am so grateful to be able to look back now and recall moments in my life like the one I had in remedial math class. I couldn't appreciate or even understand those moments at the time, because shame wouldn't stand for that! But now, as a man, I find so much comfort when I think back and recall those who did such good in my life and never fully knew the great extent to which they affected me. It is through those people that I can agree confidently that *God will never leave me or forsake me.*

As you may be remembering some difficult memories and moments, can you also recall when someone did some heavy lifting in your life and helped lift the iron coat off you? Maybe it was as simple as a compliment for your work or when you didn't like yourself—or maybe even something like Mrs. Van Hooydonk taking the time to help you understand something that everyone else assumed you already knew. I could have easily developed a belief system that all teachers were bad, especially math teachers, and were out to get me.

Part of the process of undoing shame is moving beyond a victim mentality by expecting to be victimized again and again. Yes, we may have been victimized by shame, but we are not to live as a complicit doorman and invite shame in for tea. So often we do shame's work all on our own. It feels normal and we've become accustomed to the weight and feel of the iron coat. Heck, sometimes we are so adept at doing shame's job that it takes a vacation… but it never travels very far, because it needs to keep an eye on us, just in case.

Is there someone currently in your life for whom you could do some heavy lifting? I've discovered that helping others identify and expose shame in their lives does me good as well. Real good. Much of what I have learned about defeating shame in my own life has come by counseling others. That whole "practice what you preach" saying is not just a cliché. I have seen so many people set free from the crippling bondage of shame, so I know that it can be done. But ultimately, the heaviest lifting is God's job. Only by faith can we hope for complete wholeness.

12.

Deaf, Dumb, and Blinders

ONCE SHAME FINDS A HOME, IT LIKES TO LIE (AND TELL LIES) AROUND THE HOUSE AND GET fatter and fatter. Shame grows like mold—or if you've ever been to the American South, like kudzu. Shame found a home in my heart, mind, and soul—and I have to admit, it felt normal to me. In fact, there were times when if I didn't feel shame, I didn't feel right. Shame is what some call a familiar spirit. It is so familiar to us that we either don't realize the toll it's taking as it feeds on us, or we have grown accustomed to its ubiquitous presence. It's like putting on a comfortable coat or wearing your favorite pair of jeans.

Let me give a few examples.

A family purchases a lovely new home. It has everything and appeals to every member of the family. Each child has their own bedroom, Dad has space for a media room, and Mom has an exercise room plus a kitchen with the latest technology. And to top it all off, it's got an amazing backyard! After they have settled in for a few months, they invite you and your family over for dinner and to see their new house.

You arrive with your family along with a thoughtful housewarming gift and take the nickel tour. The house is everything they said it was; you're just a tad bit jealous, but you keep that to yourself. After the tour, the children run out to the backyard and the grownups sit down for a chat while the last few minutes on the oven timer tick down.

Suddenly there is a low tremor that begins to shake the house. Though you and your spouse are startled, your hosts seem nonplused. After a few seconds of wondering if you were imagining it, the tremor grows in intensity. Your hosts offer to refill your tea. Finally a loud roaring noise can be heard as the pictures on the walls begin to shift and become unleveled. You are about to dive under the coffee table as your hosts casually straighten the paintings on their way to the kitchen for more tea. Finally you scream, "What the heck is *that?!*"

The puzzled look on the faces of your tea-refilling hosts is not only puzzling… it's downright annoying. They look at each other questioningly, as if you are crazy, and then simultaneously morph into an expression that says, *Oh yeah… right.*

You and your spouse have not yet noticed that the roaring sound has dissipated and the tremors have ebbed away, when they respond, "Oh, that's the freight train that goes by our house twice a day. The tracks are just beyond our property line out back. Look, you can see them from the kitchen."

How in the world did they not hear or feel the freight train go by? It shook the whole house, and it hurt your ears. How indeed! They didn't hear or feel it, because they had become used to or familiar with the sounds and effects from living next to train tracks. They didn't notice it until you did. And before you judge them too harshly, if you lived there as long as they have, you wouldn't notice it either. You will still hear and feel it, but you would pay no attention to it.

Similarly, have you ever been on an airplane or in a restaurant with a screaming child… that's not your screaming child? Surely the parent, who is sitting right next to them, can hear them, too. Nope! You're wrong. They have acquired Selective Hearing Syndrome, which is also what men employ while watching television. To be accurate, those parents technically hear their children; they've just tuned them out.

In the same way, shame will shake, rattle, and roll our very beings, but we may have grown accustomed to its effects and don't even notice them anymore. Shame still screams hurtful things at us, but we simply attune our hearing to accept it.

So, whenever my mother in the years would utter, at no one in particular, "I've had nothing but hell the last thirteen years!", being thirteen myself and having already attuned my ears to the voice of shame, I unknowingly, but willingly, put on another layer of the shame coat.

All in the Family

UNHEALTHY FAMILY SYSTEMS ARE AMONG SHAME'S FAVORITE BREEDING GROUNDS. IN future chapters we'll deal with other breeding grounds like school, the workplace, sports, and even church. *Not church! Say it ain't so, Steve!* Not only church, but also and especially church. But that's another chapter. And try to avoid the temptation to skip ahead.

An unhealthy family system often empowers shame (and guilt) more than any other relational system or environment. Why? Because the family system is where our identity and place/purpose in this world should be established, encouraged, and nurtured.

What is unfortunate is that a lot of today's moms and dads didn't grow up in environments that established, encouraged, and nurtured them. They don't have the plans, schematics, or blueprints to build their own healthy family system, so they lean on or default to what was modeled and reinforced, and what they are familiar with.

In a healthy family system, a parent's role is to do (but not be limited to) the following:

1. To teach and instruct.
2. To provide.
3. To establish values and set healthy boundaries.
4. To affirm identity.
5. To shape and mold character.
6. To model love for others (including their spouse).
7. To protect.
8. To repair.
9. To restore.

10. To comfort.
11. To encourage.
12. To inspire.

I believe that the vast, vast majority of parents had or have no intention of ever shaming their children, it's just that it is so dang easy to do.

Let me give you a simple, yet emotionally complex scenario. A mom and dad are dropping off their child to spend the night with the grandparents. The child is so happy and excited (because grandparents are amazing) that they tear through the house calling out to Grandma and Grandpa until they see them in the backyard where Grandpa is setting up a hammock. Without so much as an "Adios ameba" or "See ya later, alligator!" the child becomes so fully engaged with gramps and the hammock that they're not even aware that Mom and Dad are still there.

Now, before I continue, if you were the mom or dad in this scenario...

- How would you feel about your child forgetting about you?
- How would you feel toward your parents or in-laws if your child has forgot you?
- How would you feel toward your parents or in-laws for not recognizing the situation and encouraging your child to notice your existence?
- What might you say to your child?

Now back to the story.

Before the mom and dad leave, they say to their child, "Hey, aren't you going to give us a kiss or even say goodbye?" That sounds okay, right? Nope. What they said is really not okay. The mom or dad might even go on to say, "What if something happened to us tonight and you never got to see us again?" Does that sound okay? I hope you said "Nope," and you'd be correct. That's not even close to being okay.

Neither one of those statements are okay. The first is bordering on accusation, and the second creates fear. Both are highly manipulative, not to mention that they both employ guilt and shame.

Again, before continuing, if you were the grandparents in this scenario...

- How would it make you feel that your grandchild seemingly prefers you to their parents?
- What thoughts might this produce toward your own son/daughter or son/daughter-in-law?
- How would you feel if you sensed their jealousy or displeasure with their child?
- What might you say to your child?
- What might you say to your grandchild after your child left?

So far in this scenario I've only asked you to imagine yourself as one of the grownups. Can you even imagine what is going on inside of that child? This child who loves Mom and Dad *and* Grandma and Grandpa is stuck in the middle of a shame sandwich and someone needs to act like a grownup—and quickly!

This simple scenario demonstrates that there are many emotional and generational layers in our families, and therefore many, many opportunities to play right into shame's hand. When our feelings of self-worth come into question, shame is already at play and has actually been at play long before we ever went to drop of our kids at Grandma and Grandpa's house.

Typically when parents use accusation, guilt, manipulation, or shame to control, it's a learned behavior. You've probably heard the expression, "Hurt people hurt people, but healed people heal people." It may sound trite, but I've found this to be true. When people are hurt, they tend to pay it forward. Some horrifying studies show that when a child is abused by their parent(s), there is a high probability that they, too, will abuse their own children.

Abuse comes in many dastardly forms. Physical, sexual, mental, and emotional are all common forms of abuse. There is an abuse of neglect and abandonment and I would submit to you that shaming is also a form of child abuse. As a pastor for over fifteen years, I've had many people share with me that they would have rather had the spanking than the tongue-lashing they received as a child.

Notice I said spanking and not beating. Spanking should be administered with love, self-control, and with a resolution that removes all guilt. I'll talk about spanking in a later chapter. It's important to note that in order for our children to be spared from the ravages of shame, we must first become aware of and deal with any shame by which we've been ravaged.

I've had parents in my office who pride themselves for never spanking their children, but have employed shame as a tactic for discipline and punishment. Once when working with a parent, I employed a tactic that had other staff members running to my office to see if I or another person had been killed. I've since warned other staff whenever I use this tactic.

I was in my office with a father and son, and they were about as emotionally far apart as I have ever seen a father and son. The son was involved in youth ministry and the father served in other areas of the church. These were "good" church people. What was at issue was the father feeling that the son didn't respect him and the son feeling like his dad didn't love him. After talking with them and observing how they interacted with each other, I noticed a pattern. Dad would get angry and son would get frustrated. Dad used a lot of words and son shed a lot of tears.

Then I called a timeout and asked a few questions of each of them. I stood up, walked around the front of my desk, and leaned over until my nose was about an inch away from the dad's nose. I then, without using my inside voice, began to tell him what a bad father he was. I told him that he was the worst I had ever seen. I told him that he was the lamest, most miserable, no-good, rotten dad of all time. My voice was rising, as was his blood pressure. When I felt that he was just about to take a swing at me, I suddenly stopped yelling at him and whispered, "How did it make you feel when I talked to you like that?"

There was a palpable tension in the room. The father was truly about to knock my block off and was taken aback. He stammered a little, looked over at his son, wiped the sweat off his forehead, and replied, "I felt like a piece of crap!"

I leaned back and sat on my desk. Motioning to his son, I asked, "How do you think he feels when you talk to him like that?"

At first the dad was a little perplexed and confused about what had just transpired.

"Why did you look over at your son before you answered my question?" I asked the dad."

Again before he answered, he glanced over at his son. "I wanted to see if he was enjoying that or if he was laughing at me."

While grinding the dad's gears, I could see in my peripheral vision that the son was weeping. He wasn't enjoying what I had said to his father at all; in fact, he later admitted that he wanted to knock me out, too. He was crying because he loved his father and didn't like anyone speaking to him that way. And he also wept because he had heard those same words, but directed at him and coming from his father's mouth.

The father, who so desperately wanted his son's respect, already had it. But Dad had confused "obeying his commands the moment he uttered them" with respect. That's how he had shown his own father respect.

"Did you respect your father or were you afraid of him?" I asked the dad.

At first he was quite offended and got a little terse with me, but then he sat back and laughed out loud. "You know what? The truth is I was scared to death of that SOB, and I never really respected him!"

His laughter gave way to tears, and he curled up almost in a ball in the chair in which he was sitting.

Then something he didn't expect happened. While the dad was dealing with a long overdue assessment of reality, his son had quietly slipped out of his chair and was kneeling beside his dad with his right arm around his shoulder. At first the dad thought it was me who was comforting him, until he looked up and saw that it was his son. He then broke down even more. Sobbing, he begged his son's forgiveness. I left them in my office to let God finish the work He had already started in them.

A few follow-up visits later, I learned that the father was simply repeating what he had experienced growing up. His view of a father's role was to make the kid toe the line, keep his nose clean, learn that money doesn't grow on trees, and for added measure, instill in him that big boys don't cry. This dad really loved his son, but didn't know how to show it. Like his own father, he believed that going to work every day and providing a nice home and three squares a day was love enough.

He even believed he was going above and beyond his own father's example by providing "things," whatever the latest technology a teenage boy could want. But all of his hard work and providing for the family came with a hook. In return for all that the father did, he expected to receive undying respect, unquestioned obedience, and complete adherence to all his rules.

What the dad soon discovered was that rather than respect, he had felt shamed into obeying his own father. He could not recall his father ever telling him that he had done a good job. He recalled a story of when his father had asked him to mow the lawn when he was about fifteen years old. After he had finished, he told his father that the job was done and then went to take a shower. When he got of the shower, he heard the mower running and looked out his bedroom window to see his father re-mowing the lawn. He remembered how he stood there with angry tears running down his cheeks, screaming hateful things at his dad.

Now here he was, a father treating his own son the way he had hated to be treated. He came to realize that he had never dealt with the shame of his youth. He just got on with life and stuffed his feelings of shame and converted them into memories of respect for his father. Once he realized this, he began the process of forgiving his father. He didn't even expect an apology from his father, because he knew deep in his heart that his father truly loved him, just like he loved his son.

After some time, three generations began to heal. The edginess that existed between the dad and his father softened and I learned that the dad was enjoying time with his own dad. I also learned from the son that he, too, was enjoying time with his dad. No longer was his dad solely using harsh, biting words to get the son's attention or gain respect. He started adding words of affirmation, kindness, and self-control. The dad was amazed at how well his son started behaving and how quickly his grades improved in school.

I've seen this similar scenario played out many times, but in different ways. When someone grows up in a family where shame is a motivator or disciplinary method, there exists a sort of cloud or fog that no one in the family can clearly identify. There is just this feeling of dread or heaviness that comes on the family whenever they all get together. No one really talks about it as they navigate around the herd of pink elephants at family gatherings, just hoping they can get out before an argument starts.

When we operate or function in our family systems, there are usually two sets of rules: spoken rules and unspoken rules. Spoken rules are the ones like "Turn the light off when you leave a room" or "Don't stand too long in front of the refrigerator with the door open" or maybe even "Put the seat down when you're... " (I'll leave you to finish that one). Spoken rules are out in the open, and you know why other family members are upset with you when you break a rule that everyone knows.

Unspoken rules, however, are not so easily identifiable, but are undeniable when someone violates one. Unspoken rules are expectations, based upon legitimate needs, that we put on family members, but we don't verbalize them. When our needs and expectations go unmet, they become sources of increasing stress and frustration for everyone. Why? No matter how much you believe you can read other people's minds (especially your spouse's) or that they can read yours, they can't! Only God knows our thoughts. So unspoken needs will equate to unmet needs. We have to shun the UNs. If we allow the UNs to take over, we will soon be living in un-land, which may include being unmarried, unhappy, unfriended, and even unemployed.

Unspoken Rules

You may be scratching your head still, wondering what an unspoken rule is or if they even exist. They do, but it might be helpful to expound on this a little more by using an example from everyone's favorite pastime: a traffic jam.

Have you ever been in a traffic jam where everyone is trying to get into the lane that's moving? We sit in our car scanning the situation and utilizing every mirror, eyeing every potential gap between the other cars, seeking a coveted car-length advantage. Inching further and further ahead, we meander over the clearly marked white lines that define and separate the lanes, in hopes that this in-between lanes positioning will allow us to remain uncommitted to a particular lane—and at a moment's notice, to veer into the moving lane. The tension is palpable as you turn off your radio, believing that this will improve your vision. Unexpectedly, another driver sees your strategy and creates a gap for you to pull in front of them. Gratefully you wave a "thank you" from inside the car, but since you aren't sure they saw that, you flash your lights or engage your emergency flashers, and just for good measure you roll down your window to wave "thank you" to ensure they noticed your appreciation.

You now have the makings of an unspoken rule. So far, so good. Nothing bad has happened, and there are no signs of road rage. You have a car-length advantage, you unambiguously showed your gratitude to the courteous driver now positioned behind you, and in this euphoric state you decide to pay it forward. Next to you is a car straddling the white line, so you create a gap to extend the same courtesy shown to you. The driver sees the gap widen and, just as you intended, pulls their car into the lane in front of you. Mission accomplished. But suddenly you become angry.

The car, now in full view in front of you, has a bumper sticker promoting the candidate you would never vote for, a vanity license plate of your collegiate rival, and to top it all off, it's your dream car! But none of those reasons account for why you are suddenly angry. If you were angry for those reasons, you should never be allowed behind the wheel of a car again. The reason you are angry is because the other driver unknowingly violated your unspoken rule or expectation—and that rule is, "If I let you go ahead of me, you will acknowledge my act of kindness with a variety of options that include a wave, toot of your horn, or flashing of your lights." Well, they didn't wave, toot, or flash (as a comic, I am so tempted to go off on a tangent… but I will refrain).

So there you sit, stewing over your decision, wondering why that ungrateful so-and-so didn't give you even a cursory nod or toot of their horn. No, they just took advantage of your kindness and generosity and are leaving you in the dust as they seek another car-length advantage.

Ugh! you think. *Man, I can't stand those people!*

What people exactly are you referring to as *those* people? *Those* people are those who violate your rules and expectations.

If a stranger in a traffic jam can get us that upset, how much more can the people we love and care about get under our skin when they ignore our rules? Well, heck, how can others figure out our unspoken rules when we don't tell them? Guess what? They can't. We have to tell those we love, and with whom we interact, what we need exactly, instead of expecting them to understand by osmosis.

You might not even know what some of your unspoken rules are. It's rather simple. Usually our rules, spoken or unspoken, are what we expect from others, because that's often what we expect from and/or for ourselves. Who was it that was insistent that we display our gratitude to the driver behind us? It sure wasn't them. In fact, our over-exuberance may have caused them to let a few more cars in between them and us just for good measure. Because of a self-imposed expectation to show gratitude, we often expect others to reciprocate in kind.

What's really funny is that in this illustration, the driver behind us and the driver in front of us will have a totally different opinion of us. The driver in front sees us in their rearview mirror glaring at them, while motioning a "what's with you?" shrug and palms-up display. The driver behind thinks that we are overly friendly and fears we may get out of our car, run back to their car, and give them a hug! Unspoken rules or expectations are fully on display and may be obvious to everyone but us.

You see, when we value something like gratitude or courtesy, we expect that others will value gratitude or courtesy, too. At home we may value having all of our kitchen cabinet doors closed when not in use, while others seem to value letting the dishes have an unobstructed view of the stove and refrigerator.

As a side note, one of the greatest ways to affirm and encourage someone is to value what they value... within reason, of course. We don't check our integrity or morals at the doorway of encouraging others. Another way to put this is to, at minimum, appreciate what they appreciate, because they appreciate it. I can certainly appreciate someone's love for country music, even though I don't particularly care for it. I can value someone's love of cooking without having to become a master chef.

I don't have to go overboard with approval to the point of vain or meaningless flattery. I simply choose not to mock, criticize, or minimize someone else's likes and interests.

Now that we've established what unspoken rules are, we can delve deeper to discover the unspoken needs that lead to our unspoken rules.

14 ½.

Unspoken Needs

SEVERAL YEARS AGO, I HAD A PASTORAL COUNSELING SESSION WITH A COUPLE THAT HAD been married for a little over seven years. When they arrived, their body language spoke loudly and clearly that they were done with each other. So tense was their demeanor it spilled over onto me. They were incapable of being courteous to each other and were discourteous to me. I had to fight the feeling of rejection that was coming over me and resist snapping out, "Hey look, you two. I'm here to help, but if you're going to be like this, you can leave now." I am so glad I fought those feelings and kept my mouth shut.

They sat down in the two chairs that countless other couples had sat in for premarital counseling with me. Usually these two chairs, separated by a credenza, are scooted up and closer together so that the bride-and-groom-to-be can sit close enough to hold hands. The couple that now sat in those chairs seemed to appreciate the placement of the credenza.

There they sat, chairs separated, and if I remember correctly, one or both of them had turned their chair away from the other.

Oh boy, I thought to myself. *This is going to get sporty.*

After a deep breath ,I opened up the session with a prayer and then asked, "So why are we all sitting here in my office today?"

Like synchronized swimmers, they pointed at each other and exclaimed at the same time, "Ask her/him!"

I fought off the temptation to count to three and say, "You owe me a Coke!" I was again glad that I had kept my mouth shut.

To settle the tie, I asked the wife to speak first. As she began to speak, her husband's body language was screaming, as if saying, *Here we go again. Why does she always say the same thing? I am sick of this!* With eye rolls, exaggerated exhalations, and crossing his arms and legs, the husband was telling anyone with eyes that he was tired of hearing what she was saying, which in a nutshell was, "He doesn't care about me. He acts like I don't even exist. He doesn't care about my feelings. He cares more about other people than me. He always lets me down. He's too busy not letting everybody else down. It's like we've become roommates."

As she was speaking, with every sentence she became angrier with her husband and displayed increased emotions. In response, her husband began showing more indifference to her feelings and some growing agitation. At the point when I was about to ask her to allow her husband to respond to what she had been sharing, she suddenly burst into tears and screamed, as if she were a child, "And he never says 'God bless you' when I sneeze!" followed by uncontrollable weeping.

I was in a little bit of shock and looked at the husband, who looked at her and then at me while making a circular motion with his index finger by his head, which I knew meant, "See... she's crazy!" I paused for a second and what happened next surprised not only the couple, but me as well.

My first thought was to agree with the husband's assessment of his wife's mental condition. I was thinking that this poor man had married a nutcase, when I noticed her facial expression. She was mortified by her last statement and seemed embarrassed at what she had just said. Then, looking at the husband, who was still doing the "she's crazy" motion with his finger and had a slight smirk on his face—as if he was expecting me to side with him—I unexpectedly and sternly said to him, "Stop it!"

As surprised as he was at my statement m, what happened next surprised all three of us. I'm sure that at first they would have both preferred for another pastor to replace me, when I did what I'm about to tell you. And I would have agreed with them!

While the husband was wondering why I suddenly seemed to have switched teams and the wife was trying to reel in her sneeze issue, I rolled my chair over to where she was and said, "I am so sorry."

She looked at me, as if suddenly a third eye poked out of my forehead. The husband looked at me the same way. Before she could backpedal about the sneeze, I asked her, "When you were a little girl, when you sneezed, what did your father do?"

Her facial expression softened and her eyes, once filled with tears of anger, were replaced with tears of fondness. "My dad would say, 'God bless you.' Even if he was out in our garage and I was inside the house, if he heard me sneeze, he would poke his head inside and say, 'God bless you, sweetie!'"

It now became very quiet in my office.

I asked her how it had made her feel when her father did that. She went on to tell me that it made her feel loved, noticed, valued, and significant. The very things she was hoping to feel from her husband. I then asked her if she had ever told her husband about her father saying "God bless you" when she sneezed. She sniffled and, looking down at the tissue in her hand, softly said, "No."

Now here's the really surprising part of the story.

While I was intently listening to her, I hadn't noticed that her husband slid out of his chair, onto his knees, and made his way over to her chair. His expression had also softened and his eyes welled with tears of what seemed like sadness and compassion. I rolled my chair away as he knelt in front of his wife of seven years and said, "Oh babe, I'm so sorry. I had no idea."

Okay, stop the freaking presses! What in the wide world of sports is happening in my office? Just moments earlier these two were finished with each other and could hardly stand to be in the same room together. Here is Mr. She's Crazy Finger kneeling in front of and comforting his wife and Mrs. He's Got the Emotional Depth of a Teaspoon wiping tears from his eyes.

I'll tell you what's happening: an unspoken need just got spoken, and this husband was able to see his wife in a whole new light.

Allow me to explain. While these two dated and after they were married, she had a need (as everyone does) to be noticed, to be loved, to be valued, and to feel that she mattered. One of the ways she felt loved and noticed was that her father would say "God bless you" when she sneezed. But she fell in love with a man who grew up in a family that didn't say anything when someone sneezed. The first time she sneezed and her new boyfriend didn't say anything, she didn't say anything either.

As they continued to date, when she would sneeze there was no "God bless you." Even though it made her feel loved, she felt silly asking her new boyfriend if he would say those three words that translated to her as "I notice you" or "I value you," or simply "I love you."

During the time they had dated and the seven years they were married, each time her husband failed to meet an expectation she had of him to meet her needs, she buried her feelings of disappointment. Her disappointment led to feelings of resentment.

What he was experiencing was confusion. More than anything, he wanted to please his wife and make her happy. But for some reason even when he did what she wanted or expected, it was not enough.

He would accomplish a project like landscaping the backyard the way she wanted, but it was three weeks after she felt it should have been finished. He would apologize to her about something, but in her mind it was only because she had to ask him to apologize. Now he's dealing with disappointment and resentment, because he did a heck of a job on that landscaping and he was sincere in his apology.

What happened over time was they each began building a case against one another for not meeting each other's needs. She needed to feel loved and noticed and he needed to feel appreciated and admired. What seems so crazy is that their relationship got derailed by something as simple as a sneeze and was put back on track by something as simple as saying "God bless you."

I know this is an odd story, but it's true. It is both a microcosm and a metaphor for what I have witnessed in couple after couple. Far too often, the simplicity of having our legitimate needs met goes unspoken, because we feel ashamed or embarrassed to ask the very person God has divinely provided and appointed to meet those needs. Meeting your spouse's need means that you notice them, you respect their need, and most of all that you really do love them. I even know of a couple that got their relationship back on track by one of them simply closing the kitchen cabinet doors in their kitchen. Sounds silly, right? Well, it worked!

What is a need you have that you are afraid to share? Maybe it's as simple as a hug, a "God bless you," or shutting a kitchen cabinet door. Don't allow shame to keep the needs you have in the dark. You are free to have needs!

15.

It's Okay to Have Needs… in Fact, It's Normal

I'd like to offer an everyday example of how to identify and then speak up about our needs, as well as uncover how unspoken rules work.

Let's say you have a very stressful job that requires you to be on alert for most, if not all, of your day. Five days a week, eight or more hours a day, you have to focus and problem-solve until it's time to go home. On the drive home, you replay the day in your head, going over the highlights and lowlights. You're happy about what went right, but regret what went wrong. You focus in on the moment that day when you were called on the carpet in front of everyone and received a tongue-lashing lecture about your screw-up. It was so embarrassing that out of compassion for you, none of your fellow employees looked at you as they went back to their desks.

While thinking through how you're going to face your boss again and what you will do differently tomorrow, you realize that you are in your driveway. You've spent the entire drive home ruminating on a no-good-horrible-very-bad-day, and now you have to change gears quickly, stuff and suppress all the day's events, and go engage with your happy family. Turning off the ignition, you look down at your cell phone to read a text: "Hey honey, you remembered to pick up the dry cleaning before they closed, right?" You didn't. So what's another screw-up on this already no-good-horrible-very-bad-day?

Are you still with me? Are you able to identify emotionally at any level with this scenario? Do you maybe even feel something in the pit of your stomach? If so, that's a good thing, because that's how our bodies were designed. They were created to respond in this way to situations such as I just described. Read Psalm 51 and you'll see how King David's entire body reacted to what was going on in his life.

If we've lost the ability to feel anything in situations like this, it's because we've gone numb and turned on our emotional autopilot. If we don't allow ourselves to feel, we won't be able to discern what we need. People who have been shamed learn the art of going numb and turning on their emotional autopilot just to get through a moment, a situation, an entire day, or an entire life. We cannot continue on our journey out of Shame Land unless we are willing to deal with our feelings.

Okay, now back to the driveway.

In that moment of turning off the ignition, imagine that a trusted friend walks up to your car suddenly and presses a magic button that pauses everything in the world except you and your friend. Then your friend asks you, "Tell me: what do you need right now more than anything?"

What would you say? First, let me give you permission to say what you need. If you have been burdened by shame in your life, your first response to that question would be to feel that whatever you need is selfish, petty, or not a "real" need. To help prod your thinking, allow me to make a few suggestions of what you might need more than anything.

1. To not have to solve a problem.
2. To lie down.
3. To not have to talk.
4. To not have to think.
5. To eat a candy bar.
6. To give or receive a hug.
7. To have a glass of wine.
8. To be encouraged.
9. To be loved.
10. To not solve a problem *and* lie down *and* not talk *and* not think *and* eat a candy bar *and* get a hug *and* have a glass of wine *and* be encouraged *and* loved!

Well, guess what? None of those are inherently selfish, petty, or not real needs. When we battle shame, we feel that we don't have a right to any needs that may not have been approved by others. Please note that if you come home every day and lose yourself in activities or withdraw from your family, that is not healthy. That's called avoidance, which we will deal with in another chapter. Again, try to avoid skipping ahead. Let's remain focused on real and viable needs that are a result of the situation we have set up.

Okay, back to the driveway.

Your trusted friend with the magic pause button is gone, but the question remains: "What do you need right now?" What you may need is thirty minutes. Thirty minutes to not have to talk more than greeting your spouse and little ones with heartfelt affection as you come inside. Thirty minutes to not have to fix the plumbing or get gum out of Junior's hair or program the DVR. Thirty minutes to lie down, walk around your bedroom in your underwear, or stare blankly into your backyard. Thirty minutes to unwind is what you need, so that for the rest of the evening you can enjoy *being present with your family*.

Did that sound selfish to you? Well then, Jesus is one selfish Messiah. How dare He go off by Himself and leave the disciples so He could just veg out and pray. Hmm? Are you through with me? Are you ready to label me a heretic for saying such madness? If not, let's keep going. It's okay to have needs, but shame says otherwise. Shame says no while grace, love, and mercy say yes.

When is the last time you truly experienced any grace? Shame says you don't deserve it. In fact, shame says that God likes everyone… except you. The only way you might have a shot at God even remotely liking you is to deny your needs, stuff your hurts, work hard at hiding your mistakes, and most of all, tell no one.

In order to loosen shame's hold on your heart, mind, and soul, you need to be able to express your needs, and even your wants, without having to be cornered or pushed to your emotional limit. When that happens, you rarely express your needs; they explode out of you. In the aftermath, shame gladly shows up, sweeps up the mess, and gets you to stuff it all back in.

How much would your family enjoy your company if you weren't stewing about the events of the day, resenting that you can't share your needs, and getting down on yourself for not being what everyone wants you to be? It's time to verbalize your unspoken needs in order that your family can honor these need and they can then become among the spoken rules of the house. Putting these needs into words might go something like this: "Because of my job, I am under a lot of stress most of the day. When I come home, I want to enjoy being with you all, because I love you very much. I just need about thirty minutes to unwind here at home, and I'll be a lot more fun to be around." You may find that when you know this need is honored and respected, you don't need to use your thirty minutes every day, or even every week. Just knowing that you are valued, loved, and respected loosens shame's hold on you and your family system.

16.

Shame Trek... the Next Generation

SOMEONE ONCE JOKINGLY SAID, "I'M A PARENT. IT'S MY JOB TO EMBARRASS MY KIDS!" I thought that was actually quite clever and funny... when I said it. That line doesn't seem to be as clever and funny to me anymore. The reason is that somehow I forgot what it was like to be embarrassed by a parent and therefore embarrassed my own children a time or two, or maybe fifty. This chapter is for my children, especially my daughter, whom I love with all my heart and have probably embarrassed the most.

As important as it is for your needs to be recognized, honored, and respected by others, so too do the needs of your family and loved ones need to be recognized, honored, and respected by you. Please realize that if shame was a part of your family system when you were young and is ignored or left alone, it will manifest itself from one generation to another. It's important to keep in mind that shame is stealthy and may mask itself in synonyms or words related to shame. We often unwittingly operate in shaming our families. Have you ever made a family member feel guilty? Embarrassed? Distressed? Sad? All of these feelings are related in some form to shame.

Before continuing, it is absolutely vital to know the difference between being responsible *to* and responsible *for* others' (including your family's) feelings.

We cannot be, nor should we be, responsible *for* anyone else. We are and should be responsible *to* those we love. There is a huge difference. If you were to wear your favorite outfit in public and your children got embarrassed because it's "so out of style," that's not your responsibility. That's their homework, and they need to remember that you are a grownup and they can just deal with your choice of clothing.

However, if you choose to wear something specifically for the purpose of embarrassing your children… well then, my friend, that's *your* homework. And you might need to seek professional help.

You are not responsible *for* your children if they get embarrassed. At the same time, you are responsible *to* your children not to embarrass them. Shame doesn't care either way; it just wants your children to be embarrassed, for you to take the fall and your relationship to suffer.

As parents, we have the power, ability, and opportunity to intentionally and/or unintentionally shame our children. We may think we are just being funny. We may think we are just challenging and encouraging them to do better in school, their activities, or the sports in which they participate.

Have you ever been involved with little league baseball, peewee football, or dance lessons? If you have, you've either been around or are that parent who is over-the-top involved in their child's participation of said activity.

(On a side note, if you are that parent, you probably don't even realize it and think it's someone else… but the rest of us know it's you, and that's okay. No shame. I'm just making the point. I digress.)

You may have some experience with a helicopter parent, so when team rosters come out you may have found yourself praying that their child is not on your child's team. I've been guilty of giving knowing glances to other parents when "that parent" acts out or criticizes their child's play from the stands. Like the other parents in the stands, I've learned to take their behavior in stride, because after all, the game will end soon and they're not coming home with me. But do I ever stop and think about who's going home with them? That poor kid on first base, biting their bottom lip and fighting back tears.

I wish what I just described was an anomaly. I've been to my share of sporting events and dance recitals as a dad. I've also attended many of these types of events as a youth volunteer, speaker, and pastor. From what I've witnessed, these parents are everywhere.

Parents, we can embarrass our children in many obvious ways, but I want to drill down into one of those ways particularly. Embarrassing or shaming our children behind the mask of humor is so emotionally cruel. If your child expresses hurt or embarrassment at what you said or did, then all you have to do to minimize their feelings and brush off your responsibility *to* them is to claim, "I was just kidding with you. Don't be so sensitive." Now they're embarrassed and ashamed. Great parenting job!

So much of this type of shame comes from sarcasm. Sarcasm is one of shame's favorite comedy genres. The word sarcasm comes from two root words: *sark*, meaning flesh, and *kazem*, meaning to rip or tear. In other words, sarcasm means to "tear flesh." Webster's Dictionary defines sarcasm this way:

> *...to tear flesh like dogs, bite the lips in rage, speak bitterly... A keen or bitter taunt; a cutting jibe; also, irony or the use of it, esp. when contemptuous.*[3]

Synonyms include barb, cut, dart, dig, indignity, offense, insult, indignity, slight, slur, poke, putdown, etc. Related words include jeer, mock, sneer, taunt, abuse, shame, dishonor, torment, torture, attack, and disgrace.[4]

Sarcasm goes way beyond "your momma" jokes and good-natured kidding. Sarcasm has become prevalent and a seemingly accepted form of communication in our culture, especially in our youth culture... and yes, even our church youth culture. I cringed recently when a dear friend of mine jokingly referred to sarcasm as their love language.

Now, some may be thinking, *Aw, come on, Steve. Quit being so sensitive. You're a comedian, for Pete's sake. It's just a joke. It's harmless.* To those, I would encourage you to reread the definition and synonyms of sarcasm and not view this as an attack on those who have become proficient in sarcasm. Hang with me and keep reading.

A few years ago, I was speaking at a retreat. While eating dinner with a few of the families at a picnic table, I addressed the man sitting across from me with these words: "Wow! You are probably the most sarcastic person I think I've ever met." Being a comic, that is saying something. And then I just continued eating. As you can imagine, all the chatter at the picnic table came to a screeching halt. While focusing on my corn on the cob, I could feel everyone's eyes on me. After a few more awkward moments of silence, I followed up gently with, "Who hurt you?"

Before I continue with this story, if you're fairly proficient in sarcasm, I'd like for you to consider the same question I asked the man across from me. "Who hurt you?" I learned to ask this question from my dear friend Maury Buchanan, who has a way with irascible people. I've learned from Maury's gentle yet straightforward questions that some people need an invitation to take a look in the mirror... in the moment.

Now back to the picnic table.

---

3 Ibid., "Sarcasm."

4 "Sarcasm," *Merriam-Webster.com*. Date of access: January 11, 2016 (http://www.merriam-webster.com/thesaurus/Sarcasm).

It was still quiet, and for some quite uncomfortable at our table. Some folks were looking down and pushing their food around their plate with their forks in an effort to look like they weren't listening. Others simply stared at me or at the man across from me, while some looked back and forth at the two of us. I was not the least bit uncomfortable, as I had made the initial statement and asked the question with genuine love and concern for this man and a deeper concern for his wife. For the first time in all my interactions and conversations with this man, he was silent. He was not angry. He did not appear to be embarrassed. And he didn't seem to be hungry anymore.

The man sitting across from me was a leader in the church known for his wit, but this wit caused others to brace themselves when they were around him. Ironically, many of those at our table were the recipients of his wit. This leader was very intelligent, extremely talented, and quite funny, yet with all that going for him he wielded sarcasm like a sword.

Later that evening, he and I spoke privately and he told me all about how his family was known for their sarcasm and sense of humor. He also answered my question, and what he shared I will not give in detail, but suffice to say he shared times when people, especially his father, spoke negative or hurtful words to him, and at times he was embarrassed in front of others. He told me that he was estranged from his father, who was the most sarcastic man he'd ever known, and was currently estranged from one of his own sons.

As you might imagine, I had a few conversations with some of the others who were at the picnic table. One guy in particular was originally going to get up in my face about saying what I said, but after speaking to his wife, he changed his approach. He told me that he originally thought I was either mean or overly sensitive, and who the heck was I to confront his friend like that? Thank God for his wife!

When they left the dinner table, he was fuming and telling her that he was going to find me. When he looked to his wife for her approval, he discovered that she had been weeping. He asked her what was wrong, assuming that her tears were in anger toward me or sympathy for the other man. They weren't. They were angry tears, but not directed at me. They were hurt tears, but not because of me. They were because of sarcasm.

He went on to tell me that as she tearfully expressed her hurt and frustration with the man he had been about to defend, he had also hurt her.

"She told me that she can always tell when I've been around him because of the way I talk to her and even our kids after being with him," he said with his face toward the ground. He looked up with tears in his eyes. "And she told me that she feels that I don't protect or defend her when I let him say some of the things he says to her when we're together."

He had dismissed his friend's verbal jabs as him just being funny or just messing with her. What he discovered that night was that she had never been laughing.

Late that evening, and in the following days, others who had been at the same table thanked me for speaking the truth in love. I finally asked one of them, a lay leader in the church, "Why haven't any of you spoken the truth in love to him?"

His reply summed up the point I'm desperately trying to make in this chapter. "Steve, until you said something, I didn't think sarcasm was a big deal. But last night my wife and I sat up in our room until 4:00 a.m. talking about how much my sarcasm toward her and our kids rips her up. I've spent most of today talking with and apologizing to my girls. At first I thought they'd laugh it off and say it wasn't a big deal. But when I told them I wanted to ask them for forgiveness for being sarcastic, they both wept in my arms. My oldest said that she had been praying for a while that I would stop making mean and hurtful jokes and embarrassing her."

You see, sarcasm is one of those things that when we're dispensing it, it seems harmless, like it's no big deal. However, when we're on the receiving end, it can tear a hole in our hearts. Parents are responsible *to* their child to help their children's hearts become whole.

17.

Unmasking Sarcasm

THE ICONIC SYMBOL ASSOCIATED WITH THEATER IS DERIVED FROM GREEK MYTHOLOGY, which shows two white masks, one smiling and the other frowning. The masks represent two muses. The comedy mask represents the muse Thalia, who presided over comedy and idyllic poetry. Melpomene is the muse of tragedy, but was initially the muse of singing—until she was cursed because of a shameful act with her father Zeus.

Sarcasm wears both masks at the same time, hiding behind comedy while inflicting tragedy. As a comedian for more than thirty years, I was well-versed and had a well-honed knack for all things sarcastic. Add to that my lifelong battle with shame, and you have yourself a grade-A smart aleck.

Unfortunately, I have heard too many people who pride themselves on their proficiency with sarcasm. I am also saddened to know how many families use sarcasm as a primary way of interpersonal communication. Before you get irritated and think I am being overly sensitive to sarcasm, let's remember what it means—to tear flesh. Do you really want to communicate in such a way that it tears at a person's soul? Sure, they may have laughed when you said what you said, but that's the cultural norm we have been trained to accept.

We teach our sons that boys don't cry and tell our daughters to stop being so sensitive. Granted, there are times when our children can react in an overly emotional manner, which requires a lesson in self-control rather than a blanket rule that applies to any and all situations. If your fifteen-year-old son is crying because Mom made broccoli casserole instead of macaroni and cheese, by all means deal with a self-control (or maybe entitlement) issue. But if that same fifteen-year-old son were in his room crying because something happened at school that wounded him, it would be cruel to demand that he dry his tears and for you to declare "Men don't cry" without even asking what happened.

As a side note, most teenagers are reluctant to tell parents much of anything, especially something deeply personal. If you are patient, you'll probably hear what's going on while they're talking to a friend.

When it comes to daughters, it's a little more complicated. Daughters are by nature more in tune with their feelings than sons. And it's culturally more acceptable for a daughter to cry about anything. This can lead to an occasional outburst of overly emotional responses from our teenage daughters when they're watching a Twilight marathon on TV. Please oh please, feel free to be a tad bit irritated and then teach a little self-control or lesson on reality.

Daughters have a capacity for genuine sensitivity for others that can cause them to weep deeply. In these moments, insisting that they stop being so emotional equates to insisting that they stop being so compassionate. Again, each child and situation is different, and that is why blanket rules don't always apply. Looking both ways before you cross the street is a fairly trustworthy blanket rule, though.

So with a culture that encourages us to cover up our true feelings and emotions, shame gives sarcasm a free pass. It allows us to be passive aggressive, masked with humor.

While facilitating a church's staff retreat, it was plain to see that the staff's overriding way of communication was through sarcasm. At one session, a staff member arrived late and was met with a chorus of comments like "Nice of you to join us" and "If you can't come on time, just come when you can." Everyone had a good laugh, except for the tardy staff member, who strained out a smile. Your work, family, or social environment may be similar, and you may wonder, what's the big deal?

Stop for a moment and think about the last time you used sarcasm or when it was used on you. How did it make you feel when you delivered it? Most likely you felt empowered, smart, or witty. Now how did it feel when it was used on you? More than likely you felt minimized dismissed, embarrassed, or angry.

Now, back to the tardy staff member. What if the reason they were late was that they received a phone call on their way to the session that informed them of a family tragedy. While processing this sudden bad news, they walk into a room of coworkers and are immediately met with hoots and catcalls about being late. Ouch! You see, no one in the room knows why that staff member arrived late. And even if they have a history of being late to meetings, no one is clairvoyant enough to know why they are late this time.

Though very talented, this particular staff had a flaw or chink in their armor that was causing some unintended wounds from friendly fire. Even as each staff member would insist that they were only joking, they were really frustrated. But rather than deal with the issue appropriately, their staff culture became passive aggressive, using humor to shame others in order to control them or change their behavior. How could they have handled this situation more appropriately? Using this staff meeting as the scenario, please allow me to offer some ideas.

First, don't assume you know why someone is late to a meeting. You cannot read minds or know a person's heart. Even if they are always late, you still don't know why.

Second, offer concern and/or compassion to the tardy staff member, erring on the side of grace and mercy. So instead of being met with sarcastic comments, they are met with "Hey, is everything okay?" or "We were getting concerned about you. Glad you're here safely."

Third, if they are habitually late for meetings, don't be a lazy leader! Initiate a closed-door, private meeting to address the staff member's habitual tardiness and what your expectations are concerning promptness.

When the staff members implemented the strategies I suggested above, they were surprised by some unexpected results. A result that affected everyone was that their anxiety prior to staff meetings greatly decreased. Their meetings took on a more positive atmosphere, which led to them being more open and honest with each other. Another result was that the habitually tardy staff member became regularly punctual. When the others met his tardiness with kindness, he took it to heart and decided to honor his fellow staff members with promptness. He later realized that part of his tardiness was his way of being passive aggressive.

So what are we actually doing when we employ sarcasm? We are putting the tragedy mask over our face, and then the comedy mask over tragedy. We hide hurtful and unredemptive words with a smile. Wise King Solomon addresses sarcasm this way: *"Like a maniac shooting flaming arrows of death is one who deceives their neighbor and says, 'I was only joking!'"* (Proverbs 26:19)

The Apostle Paul says, *"Nor should there be obscenity, foolish talk or coarse joking, which are out of place, but rather thanksgiving"* (Ephesians 5:4).

Sarcasm is undeniably powerful. It has the power to:

- Make us feel or look stupid.
- Minimize us.
- Shut us up.
- Make us believe that we are being overly sensitive or minimize when we have been hurt.

If sarcasm is a regular part of the way you communicate and interact with others, you may want to go back and think about how sarcasm makes you feel when directed toward you.

Shame and sarcasm are two peas in a pod and enjoy working as a team. Once you separate them, they begin to lose their hold on you. Oh, and did I mention that sarcasm has a cousin? Whereas sarcasm is often meted out with subtlety, mockery is about as subtle as a bag of hammers and typically cloaked in humor.

Mockery

No one likes to have their words repeated back to them, unless they ask you to or if you are cooing with a little baby. To test my theory, put down this book, find someone, and start repeating every word that they say for the next five minutes. I'll wait here until you get back.

Back so soon? Bet you either didn't do it—or within about 60 seconds of doing that exercise, you realized you were in imminent danger of having a dirty sock shoved into your mouth. In either case, I'm glad you're still here.

Mockery is another tactic of shame, but it's not as overt as sarcasm. Mockery is usually cloaked in good-natured teasing, pestering, or trifling. Mocking is something that can be done without words—an eye roll is often sufficient.

Mockery is defined as

1. Insulting or contemptuous action or speech; derision; ridicule. 2. A subject or occasion of derision or sport. 3. Mimicry; imitation; now, an insincere, contemptible, or impertinent imitation. 4. Ridiculously useless action.[5]

So far, I am not a fan. Yet mockery is commonly used as a form of humor in our culture. *Saturday Night Live, Mad TV, Second City TV,* and other television series base most of their skits on mocking politicians, athletes, celebrities, special interest groups, and religious organizations. When these skits are done in the spirit of all-good humor, the person whom the skit is about, watching from the comfort of their own living room, would probably have a good laugh. However, when the skit employs mockery (rather than parody), I don't think the subject watching in their living room will feel that imitation is the sincerest

---

5 *Webster's Collegiate Dictionary,* Third Edition of the Merriam Series, "Mockery" (Springfield, MA: G. & C. Merriam Co., 1928).

form of flattery. Most likely they will feel embarrassed rather than flattered, and defensive rather than affirmed.

I would dare to say that social media has changed our culture as much as the invention of the light bulb and automobiles. Words like posting, tweeting, and following, have taken on whole new meanings. And new words have emerged like selfie, hashtag, blogging, and unfriending.

It won't take much searching on the Internet to find story after story about politicians, athletes, celebrities, special interest groups, and religious leaders who have been lampooned on TV or in print and within moments are tweeting their response. What social media has unintentionally uncovered is the raw and unfiltered reaction people have to being made fun of, and no matter who you are, no one likes to be made fun of.

How many defensive and angry tweets have you seen from the likes of Kanye West, Kim Kardashian, Alec Baldwin, and Lena Dunham? We assume that these celebrities are surely prepared for and used to criticism (mockery), because after all, they're celebrities, right? Celebrity or not, no one—no matter how much they say "I don't care what other people think"—likes to be mocked. And when we mock someone, it can also be a very subtle form of judgment.

In its various forms, mockery is referred to in the Bible at least seventy-two times and is a form of ridicule directed especially against individuals with the purpose of humiliating them. Scripture refers to mockers as arrogant, unrighteous, and foolish. Beginning in Genesis and all the way to the cross, mockers are prevalent. Proverbs warns against mockery as it does against greed, lust, and falsehood. The psalmists recount those who would mock God. And what is God's response to mockery?

God's response to mockery is best summed up in 2 Chronicles:

But they mocked God's messengers, despised his words and scoffed at his prophets until the wrath of the Lord was aroused against his people and there was no remedy.

—2 Chronicles 36:16

Apparently mockery arouses God's wrath. Sometimes I want to know what God doesn't like as much as I want to know what He does like. That way, as I try to please Him, I know what to avoid. In the Psalms, it says,

Blessed is the one who does not walk in step with the wicked or stand in the way that sinners take or sit in the company of mockers…

—Psalm 1:1

This verse seems to suggest that there is even a blessing for those who avoid mockery. After all, it is the wise man that holds his tongue, right?

Again, several verses deal with mockery, but here are just a few:

- Sarah is angered when Ishmael mocks Isaac (Genesis 21:9).
- Mockery arouses God's anger (2 Chronicles 36:16).
- Job is overcome by the hostility of those mocking him (Job 17:2).
- A blessed man will avoid the company of mockers (Psalm 1:1).
- Asaph is troubled by those who mock God (Psalm 74:10).
- Isaiah warns that mockery will lead to greater bondage (Isaiah 28:22).
- Jesus is mocked while on the cross (Luke 23:36).

According to the Bible, those who mock or engage in mockery…

- Are described as proud or arrogant:

The arrogant mock me unmercifully, but I do not turn from your law.

—Psalm 119:51

The proud and arrogant person—"Mocker" is his name—behaves with insolent fury.

—Proverbs 21:24

- Cause strife, quarrels, and are insulting:

Drive out the mocker, and out goes strife; quarrels and insults are ended.

—Proverbs 22:10

- Resent correction and refuse counsel:

Mockers resent correction, so they avoid the wise.

—Proverbs 15:12

Fools mock at making amends for sin, but goodwill is found among the upright.
—Proverbs 14:9

• Are ultimately punished:

Penalties are prepared for mockers, and beatings for the backs of fools.
—Proverbs 19:29

Do not be deceived: God cannot be mocked. A man reaps what he sows.
—Galatians 6:7

Those who are mocked in the Bible include God the Father, Job, God's prophets or messengers, the disciples, and the Lord Jesus Christ. Mockery has been around from the beginning, so it comes as no surprise that it's still very much alive and well.

Today, mockery is so deeply ingrained in our culture that it's really difficult to notice sometimes. Using satire as a comic is a very fine line because satire can be just shy of mockery. The very best comics I know walk this verbal tightrope and the result is always the same; people laugh, not at the expense of another, but at themselves.

I'm learning to walk that tightrope.

As a comic, I know how easy it is to employ mockery as part of a routine, but like refraining from using vulgar language, I am also learning to refrain from using mockery. It's called self-discipline. I wish I were a model of that discipline a hundred percent of the time. It's been so long ago that I can't remember the last time I used a naughty word onstage. Unfortunately, I can remember the last time I let my guard down and used mockery. My hope is that one day I will not be able to remember the last time I did that. So to that end, every night I walk onstage with this silent prayer on my lips:

Blessed is the one who does not walk in step with the wicked or stand in the way that sinners take or sit in the company of mockers...
—Psalm 1:1

But It's a Tradition!

Not long ago, I was a guest speaker at a youth camp. The youth pastor and his wife, because of their genuine love for the students in their care, impressed me. Though he had been in youth ministry many years, he had only been at this church for a few months, but his impact was evident. The week had gone well, and I was the speaker for the last evening session on Friday night. I had already spoken twice that week and had a feel for where the students were in their journey with Jesus. But when the evening session started, I became disturbed by something that was a tradition in this youth ministry. The youth pastor had unwantedly inherited it when he came on staff. My skin began to crawl. I became so unnerved that I had to leave the room and go downstairs to gather myself.

Once out of the room, the tradition continued to play out upstairs, but I began feeling things I hadn't felt in years. I felt the familiar pangs of fear and shame that were associated with being molested as a young boy, and then later when I was in high school. I began quoting the scriptures I knew would help reset my mind and comfort my spirit.

We demolish arguments and every pretension that sets itself up against the knowledge of God, and we take captive every thought to make it obedient to Christ.
—2 Corinthians 10:5

I began pacing and praying out loud, quoting that and other verses that had to do with forgiveness, self-control, and our Father's comfort. Prayer and the power of His Word sustained me that night.

Now, before you imagine horrific scenarios happening upstairs at the youth camp, you might be surprised about what had unnerved me: a video. There was no blood, no guts, and no violence, not even a spooky monster, just a sleeping camper, an adult leader, and a video camera. The video was intended to be funny and elicited laughter among the youth and adults. But not everyone was laughing, including me.

What was being shown were several different students being awakened from a deep sleep, and before they were fully awake, they were asked questions or given things to eat, all while being recorded. I grant you that this sounds like a humorous idea for a camp video; however, I'd like to break this down to help you understand why I was so disturbed.

When parents send their children to a camp, especially a church camp, there is an expectation that their child is in good hands—hands that will challenge and not harm, comfort but not coddle, and encourage but not embarrass. In the video, each student was presented in a scenario that showed them in a negative light, far from their best. They were disheveled, confused, and appeared to be unintelligent. Proverbs says,

> *When you lie down, you will not be afraid; when you lie down, your sleep will be sweet. Have no fear of sudden disaster or of the ruin that overtakes the wicked, for the Lord will be at your side and will keep your foot from being snared.*
> —Proverbs 3:24–26

Allow me to repeat this verse.

> *When you lie down, you will not be afraid; when you lie down, your sleep will be sweet. Have no fear of sudden disaster or of the ruin that overtakes the wicked, for the Lord will be at your side and will keep your foot from being snared.*
> —Proverbs 3:24–26

There was nothing safe or sweet about what I saw as each camper's sleep was interrupted and disturbed. Each one stared blankly into the camera, trying to figure out what was going on. When that moment, captured on video, was played on the big screens for everyone to see, I pondered how safe that teenager—who was most likely already dealing with insecurity—felt at that moment.

To be fair, to some it could appear that I'm making a mountain out of a molehill. After all, it's just a practical joke and a church tradition. However, what if a student in the video, or one simply watching it, were taken back to a moment similar to this, but not for a funny video. It was my (and countless others that I've ministered to) experience that when I was sound asleep, the molestations occurred. I have vague memories of people in my bed and other more distinct memories. The vague memories are those near waking moments when I realized that someone was touching me and the person would stop once they realized I was waking up. The distinct memories are ones where I fully awoke, but was paralyzed with fear and pretended to be asleep and would roll over or curl up in a ball. That desire to curl up in a ball came flooding back as I watched these campers being accosted in their sleep. Yes, I said "accosted," and you're lucky I'm not using a few choice words to go along with it. It made me want to cuss then… and now.

Let's put the shoe on the other foot. What if it were your child who was in the video? What if the attempt to be funny involved disturbing your child's sleep and made them the subject of ridicule? Is your pulse rising a bit? I hope so, because if there is nothing about this scenario that evokes even the slightest bit of parental protection in you, I would like to see you in my office asap!

Shame's favorite jokes are practical ones, although I've never seen what is so practical about them. Webster's defines a practical joke as a "prank intended to trick or embarrass someone or cause physical discomfort."[6] Hmmm, I don't know about you, but that's not the kind of joke I would like played on me. And my wife and I never sought a youth ministry for our kids that employed practical jokes in their traditions.

It may be that some reading this are rolling their eyes and are a bit exasperated that I wasted so much time on this story. It may be that some reading this are experiencing some anxiety and even choking back tears. At this point I'd like to rely on the wisdom (or skills for living life honorably) in the book of Proverbs:

A fool finds pleasure in wicked schemes, but a person of understanding delights in wisdom.

—Proverbs 10:23

Fools mock at making amends for sin, but goodwill is found among the upright.

—Proverbs 14:9

Even in laughter the heart may ache, and rejoicing end in grief.

—Proverbs 14:13

---

6 "Practical joke," *Merriam-Webster.com*. Date of access: January 11, 2016 (http://www.merriam-webster.com/dictionary/practical%20joke).

Folly brings joy to one who has no sense, but whoever has understanding keeps a straight course.

—Proverbs 15:21

Like a maniac shooting flaming arrows of death is one who deceives their neighbor and says, "I was only joking!"

—Proverbs 26:18–19

I don't feel the need to interpret the scriptures listed above; they speak for themselves, and it is the ministry and role of the Holy Spirit to bring revelation, conviction, or correction. Our responsibility is to hear the Word, not harden our hearts—to be doers of what it says. The Apostle Paul dealt with this type of joking with the church at Ephesus. He admonishes the Ephesians with these words:

But among you there must not be even a hint of sexual immorality, or of any kind of impurity, or of greed, because these are improper for God's holy people. Nor should there be obscenity, foolish talk or coarse joking, which are out of place, but rather thanksgiving.

—Ephesians 5: 3–4

I'd like to end this chapter by asking whether you were ever the subject of a practical joke or if you ever played one on someone else—or both. Can you remember what the joke was? Can you recall how you felt? Can you recall how the other person reacted or responded? You may not have known the definition of a practical joke back then, but now that you do, what is an appropriate response?

Not to feel shame, but to be free of it! First, ask God to forgive you for any shame you may have caused another with a practical joke. Secondly, ask God to give you the strength to forgive others who played a joke on you that caused you embarrassment, pain, or discomfort. You might be surprised that something that happened in the third grade is flashing before your mind's eye.

Remember, if any of us lacks wisdom, we can cry out for it, and God will give it to us without finding fault (James 1). Is there someone you need to forgive? Is there someone you need to call and ask forgiveness from? Ask your Father, who knows your needs even before you ask, for wisdom and revelation as to what He would have you do.

20.

Squeaky

I was never one for practical jokes, even before knowing the definition. I do recall one played on me by one of my dearest friends. I recall it often, not because of any unforgiveness, but because of the feeling it produced in me. Every now and again I experience that same feeling and it takes me back to that moment. I have to resist replaying that moment over and over in my head. I'll deal with that topic in an upcoming chapter.

While living in Nashville, Tennessee from 1986 through 2002, I was blessed to live among what I would call my tribe. Nashville is home to an eclectic array of entertainers, not limited to just the country music genre. Various musicians, actors, writers, comedians, dancers, producers, and directors... you name it and Nashville has it. And while living in Nashville, it wasn't uncommon for a friend to ask you to perform at an event they were hosting. So when I got the call to do a few minutes of stand-up at a friend's husbands-only Tupperware® party, I willingly obliged. Unbeknownst to me was that I was being set up for a practical joke.

At first I thought that they couldn't hear me or didn't know that I was supposed to be doing comedy. I tried another bit. No response. I started to panic and tried to engage some guys by name to get a rapport going. As I asked a guy his name, he turned his head and started talking to a guy next to him. Just like that night several years ago, my face is getting red with embarrassment as I type this. That night I went from being embarrassed to angry. Actually, I was way beyond angry... I was pissed off!

Shame will do that to you. You can feel embarrassed one minute and the next be enraged, which is then followed by embarrassment again for getting angry. I hate shame. After a few more valiant and futile attempts to get a laugh, I gave up and slunk away to the punch bowl praying that it was spiked with Prozac. I was trying to figure out how to leave with a shred of dignity when another friend of mine who was at the party came over to get some punch, too. What he told me almost made me punch him.

The practical joke being played was that prior to me arriving, the person who had invited me instructed everyone at the party to not laugh, no matter what, at anything I said and to begin ignoring me after a few minutes and start talking to each other. By the way, I can feel my back sweating as I type this. Believe me, there is nothing more gruesome for a comic than to bomb, to stand in front of a crowd while no one is laughing, and it's even worse if they are ignoring you.

Like I said before, I am and never was one for practical jokes, but I did my share of shaming others, even as a kid. In a previous chapter we explored the power of nicknames. Most people I know either have, or at one time in their life had, a nickname. Some are endearing and some you have to endure. I can remember one particular nickname from high school that still sends a shudder down my spine. It wasn't my nickname, and it wasn't the nickname of the school bully. It was the nickname of one of the most persecuted kids I ever knew.

How the nickname came to rest on him is kind of fuzzy in my recollection, I think partly because I helped create it. Squeaky. That's it, just Squeaky—kind of innocuous, but highly effective in producing shame on an adolescent just trying to make it through the hierarchy of upper classmates and the cool scene, of which you were either in or very out. If recollection serves me, the name emerged from band class, a clarinet, and a kid's valiant attempt to make a note come out of it.

Though the nickname was bestowed upon him in high school, I can remember him being picked on all through elementary and junior high school. One time in particular while he was still in elementary school—I believe we were in the fifth grade—a pack of us chased him down a street until he made the tactical error of trying to find sanctuary in a phone booth. Yes, a phone booth. Remember those? For those who have never seen one, it's a glass enclosure measuring three feet by three feet with a two-foot opening along the bottom. Good enough for Clark Kent to change into Superman, but not the best choice for Squeaky that day. We must have looked like great whites going after a diver in a shark cage. (I feel remorse even as I write this.)

Finally, someone bigger than us showed up, and we fled like the pack of rats that we were, yelling out testosterone-induced threats as we scampered away. Once I was a safe distance from Squeaky's deliverer, I hid behind a tree and watched as he coaxed Squeaky out of the phone booth, walking with him for several blocks. Since everyone fled in different directions, I was standing there all alone when it hit me. I didn't even know why we were chasing him! It just sort of happened. A thought came to me that the guys chasing him would have been chasing me if there weren't a Squeaky around.

Maybe I ought to have left Squeaky alone; then again, it was better for him to be the one hiding in a phone booth than me. The fear of being the one picked on was enough for me to keep my good intentions to myself and continue shaming Squeaky through high school. I hadn't thought of Squeaky in later years—in fact, I never thought much about anything that dealt with school.

Several years ago, I was asked to speak at a Christian school's chapel service back in my hometown. I was familiar with the school because it was part of my favorite church in the community; it had two baseball diamonds on its property. Speaking to fifth and sixth graders may not be everyone's first choice, but I always enjoy that age group. As I told my testimony of how I came to believe in Jesus as Messiah, I noticed a familiar face in the audience. I was so caught off-guard that I began rambling and not making much sense, until I decided to stop and address the person in front of the students.

"Mr. Coram," I said, looking at the familiar face, "would you stand up please?"

As he stood, the students giggled that the speaker actually knew one of the teachers.

"Mr. Coram, would you please forgive me for picking on you all through school, and especially for when I helped chase you into the phone booth when we were in the fifth grade?"

Tears filled his eyes as he nodded yes, and I could only assume he was recalling the pain that I had inflicted. I confessed to those students that day how awful a person I was before Jesus saved me. It was a great visual aid having Mr. Coram standing there, as the students witnessed my remorse and his pain. Grade-school children have a depth of feeling and understanding that I would not have known had I not witnessed it myself.

After chapel, Mr. Coram approached me with a warm embrace and tears still in his eyes. I began to blurt out, "I'm sorry I made you cry by remembering the phone booth thing, I—"

"No, no, I'm not crying about that. I was crying because you are a Christian now. I've been praying for you for years."

That last statement chilled me. He had prayed for one of the biggest jerks he probably ever knew and now saw the fruit of his labor. If you asked me before that day what kind of prayers Squeaky would be praying for me, I would have told you prayers that leprosy would be in every generation of my family starting with me. But Squeaky knew something I didn't know while I was growing up: never return cursing with cursing; return cursing with blessing.

How could a loving, righteous God listen to the prayers of one of His children in the midst of enduring incredible persecution, blessing those who persecuted him, and not be pleased enough to answer their request? What a revelation! A kid who had a perfect right to pray David-like prayers of "Destroy my adversaries" and "Wipe them from the face of the earth" chose to pray for my salvation. Sometimes God's principles don't seem very fair, until we are on the receiving end of the blessing.

It's been hard in the past for me to pray for my enemies and for those who caused me to feel shame. Yet here was a guy who had prayed for his enemy who caused him shame. At times it's hard for me to forgive, yet I want to be forgiven the moment I ask, right there on the spot. Unforgiveness is a tormenter.

In Matthew 18, Jesus tells a parable of a man who was forgiven a debt to a king that he could never repay. Upon his release, he met a man who owed him a debt that was much smaller. Instead of being grateful and remembering that he had been forgiven a huge debt, he refused to give the man who owed him a minuscule amount of money, and he had him thrown in prison until the debt was repaid. When the king heard of this, he summoned the man whom he forgave and asked, "Didn't I forgive you? Why didn't you forgive?"

In anger his master handed him over to the jailers to be tortured, until he should pay back all he owed.

—Matthew 18:34

At the end of the parable, Jesus looked at His disciples and stated, "This is how my Heavenly Father will treat each of you if you do not forgive your brother in your heart."

After all those years, Squeaky refused to let bitterness and unforgiveness take him captive. He eluded their grasp by choosing to bless and not curse.

Shame creeps onto us and comes off us in layers. Maybe this story revealed another layer of shame's influence in your life. As you read, you might have remembered an incident when you were the one being chased and harassed. Perhaps you recalled a time when you were one of those doing the harassing. In order to loosen shame's grip and begin to peel it off, we must embrace the fact that forgiveness is a lifelong journey. I invite you to go a layer deeper in being released from shame through the power of forgiveness.

Are there any names or faces from your past that made your stomach flutter or cause your back to tingle and make you shutter at the thought of them? It could be that even though you haven't thought about them in years and have "gotten over it, maybe… just maybe… you aren't as over it as you believed.

Conversely, are there any names or faces from your past that cause you to feel sorrowful about your behavior or actions toward them? Is there a place in the pit of your stomach that makes you wish you could go back and undo all the hurt you caused? Hold on to that feeling while reading on.

I wonder if somewhere, somehow, the people who hurt you might be feeling the same way. Perhaps they have also matured, like you, and have many sad regrets about the way they behaved and acted toward you. This thought, combined with your own sorrow, might help you to forgive those you never, ever thought you could or would ever forgive.

Name Calling

NAMES ARE IMPORTANT. THAT'S WHY MOST PARENTS TAKE TIME TO SEARCH OUT NAMES and their meanings before settling on a name for their new baby. Not only that, parents also need to explore how the name they choose may become fodder for bullies.

When Kathy and I were in the process of naming our children, we thought through every potential unwanted nickname that could be derived from what we chose. I am glad to report that the worst nickname that other kids came up with was Graham Cracker, for our son Graham. Granted, some kids can be very creative and come up with a combination parents never thought through, but sometimes parents make it way too easy for the playground bully.

I have a friend whose parents named him Harold. That's a nice enough name, don't you think? However, they apparently didn't do the math when it came to putting Harold and their last name together. Their last name is Pitts, and when you are named Harold, you soon become known as Harry, and to that end my friend endured his school years as Hairy Armpits.

As with having an unwanted nickname, I cringe whenever I hear someone call someone a name that's not his or her given or intended name. I have no issue with nicknames as names of endearment, or when a Robert is called Bob, Samantha is referred to as Sami, or a Jonathan is called John. What's troubling is when someone is referred to as Crap for Brains, Sleaze-ball, or Retard. On the surface, name-calling appears to be innocuous, playful, or harmless. Trust me, it's not.

Before going any further with this train of thought, I encourage you to not go looking for demons under every doily. This is yet another touchy subject matter that will require wisdom and the application of the principle of Ecclesiastes 7:18:

It is good to grasp one and not let go of the other. Whoever fears God will avoid all extremes.

There are extremes we can go to with everything under the sun. What follows is food for thought to consider how we use words or the names we call people that are negatively descriptive.

We are not called to be the nickname police and hand out citations for name-calling (unless you are a kindergarten teacher, and then by all means feel free to nip that in the bud). But we are responsible to guard our own hearts and tongues.

In the Bible, names seem to be taken very seriously. You'll find that God has all kinds of names, and even one that was unpronounceable. When recording biblical history, not only did historians write names, but also their meaning. Here are just a few examples:

- Adam: man.
- Eve: to breathe, or to live.
- David: beloved.
- Elisha: my God is salvation.
- Emmanuel: God with us.
- Esther: star.
- Habakkuk: embrace.
- Hannah: favor or grace.
- Isaac: he laughs.
- Isaiah: Yahweh is salvation.
- Paul: humble.

While these names have meanings that are positive, there are also names that have meanings that are... well, less than desirable:

- Jael: mountain goat.
- Jezebel: not exalted.
- Jabez: trouble.
- Jacob: supplanter.

What is important to note is that words and names mean things. The old singsong phrase "Sticks and stones may break my bones, but names will never hurt me" may sound correct, until we hold it up to the light of scripture.

The tongue has the power of life and death, and those who live it will eat its fruit.
—Proverbs 18:21

But I tell you that everyone will have to give account on the day of judgment for every empty word they have spoken
—Matthew 12:36

Be devoted to one another in love. Honor one another above yourselves.
—Romans 12:10

That word "honor" in Romans 12:10 is often lost in western culture. I have several Asian friends who were born and raised here in the West. They are uncomfortable with the lack of honor they see outside of their homes. I've learned more about honor from these friends than I ever learned in school, and later in church life. You think I'm exaggerating that last part?

Quick survey. Does your youth minister, pastor, director, or whoever instill a culture of honor in your church's youth ministry, or do they simply preach about honoring Mom and Dad in an occasional sermon? It's been my experience that the latter is often the case. In my experience, a lot of new youth ministers were not trained or equipped during Bible College to understand the principle of honor. Oftentimes they are taught philosophy, the rules and regulations of the church, the history of the church, and the books of the Bible... in order. So how can they model what's not been modeled for them?

Honor is something uniquely God. Notice how the Father honors the Son and the Son honors the Holy Spirit. Jesus continually gave glory and honor to His Father for all His signs, wonders, and wisdom. He even went so far as to tell His disciples that it was better for Him to go (to the cross) so that Someone even better could not only come alongside, but also dwell within them beginning on the day of Pentecost. The Father honors His Son and seats Him at His right hand, and the Holy Spirit honors the Father by empowering the church to do His will, crediting the Son by doing all things in the name of Jesus. Man, I really hope that just made sense to you.

When we honor others above ourselves, we don't call them unbecoming names. We don't use the power of words to harm or shame, we utilize the power of words (and names) to strengthen, comfort, and encourage others. At least, that's what the Bible says.

In case you were wondering, I discovered that God has a few nicknames (names of endearment) for us. They always come from a place of love, affection, and honor. Here are some of the nicknames He has for you. Beloved. Blessed. Chosen. Child. The Father also has a few names of endearment for His son. One in particular is one that He keeps to Himself.

> *His eyes are like blazing fire, and on his head are many crowns. He has a name written on him that no one knows but he himself.*
>
> —Revelation 19:12

It seems to me that God takes names very seriously.

I encourage you to look inward, and again resist the temptation to become the word police or confront people who are exercising their right of free speech. Simply ask yourself, "Are the words (names) I use for other people honoring or are they 'idle'" (Matthew 12:36, KJV)? When I speak, do I cause harm or bring health?" My hope is that this chapter is not about becoming politically correct, but becoming wise about our words and how they affect others.

What about your name? What does it mean? Ask God to bring revelation beyond just its definition. Maybe like Jacob, Simon, or Saul, God will speak a new name over those who daily bear the pain of a name. I can imagine a son or daughter who bears a parent's name but never received a day of love or affection from the one they were named after—so their own name could be a bitter reminder, and maybe even feels like they cannot break the mold their parent began. Jacob was renamed Israel, Jesus renamed Simon as Peter, and Saul is now known as Paul.

22.

Unasked-for Advice

As I mentioned early on, shame may attach itself to words that others speak, but they never intended to be shaming. It can attach itself to well-intended advice, especially advice that we didn't ask for. To be fair, we should be careful not to become easily offended when others offer unasked-for counsel. My experience is that most often they are earnest and believe that they are helping. This should also serve as a reminder the next time we offer the same unasked-for counsel. In every relationship, there should be healthy boundaries that help us discern the difference between well-intentioned advice and a controlling busybody.

On the drive home from a speaking engagement, I grew tired of what my iTunes and satellite radio had to offer. I decided to catch up on some relationships and took full advantage of my car's hands-free feature. My car utilizes voice recognition that allows me to use voice commands like Captain Kirk on the bridge of the Starship Enterprise. It's a young boy's dream come true, and don't even get me started on my conversations with Siri. She gets me!

After catching up with the person on the other end of the phone about what was going on in my life, instead of catching me up on theirs, they began giving me advice about what I should do concerning some of what I had shared. The back of my neck grew hot and the feeling continued all the way down my spine. All of a sudden, as I'm driving on a major interstate, that feeling took me all the way back to a memory from the sixth grade. I was standing in front of the class at the blackboard, chalk in hand, with Mrs. Bullard staring me down as I tried to solve an equation to which I knew the answer, yet I stood there frozen out of fear of failure.

I shook off this image to reengage and tried to interject some thoughts concerning the advice I was receiving. I tried to mention that I had already done some of what was being offered. But after a few failed attempts, I gave up and just listened to the well-intentioned lecture. The feeling of shame was lifting, but I couldn't shake the feeling that I was being criticized. Then it hit me. When others give me advice that I haven't asked for, it can come across as criticism or disapproval. Proverbs 26:17 says that if we meddle in the life of another, it's like grabbing a stray dog by the ears.

The back of my neck started to burn again, but for another reason. I began recalling times when I offered advice that wasn't asked for.

I was embarrassed as I remembered when I had insinuated myself into situations that I had no role in, almost as if I were saying, "Why would I live in my life when I can live in yours?" I came to realize that so often I felt compelled to say something rather than having something to say, which goes back to the lesson I learned later in life to share what I'm learning and not what I *know*.

I've learned that when people are in crisis or have an issue, whether by their own doing or not, they are more open to counsel and advice when it's accompanied with empathy rather than judgment, anger, or frustration. Don't get me wrong; it's really easy for me to become frustrated and angry when repeat offenders of self-inflicted crises or issues come a-whining, but I'm not talking about that. I'm talking about those of us who feel the need to speak into or comment on situations that we have no business sniffing around.

Jesus met a woman who was a total wreck and was a repeat offender in picking the wrong man. He knew in great detail all of this woman's failures and self-inflicted issues, yet He doesn't offer advice; He asks her a question. Most of Jesus' conversations start with a question, not because He is looking for information, but for relationship. This woman's encounter with Jesus uplifted her to the point where she not only took His words to heart, she wanted others to come listen to Him as well (John 4:1–30).

When someone is sharing a crisis or issue with us, maybe we should wait until they ask for advice or, like Jesus, ask them a question or two. Ah yes… and remember empathy. If we don't, inadvertent shame is often the result. Because when we give unasked-for advice or counsel, it almost always comes across as criticism. If we offer advice well, we may also uplift others to the point where they encourage others in crisis to talk with us. And isn't that just what Jesus would want us to do?

23.

Shame Attacks

...for he is the kind of person who is always thinking about the cost. "Eat and drink," he says to you, but his heart is not with you [and he is grudging the cost].
—Proverbs 23:7

IN A PREVIOUS CHAPTER, I PROMISED TO SHARE SOME PERSONAL EXPERIENCES OF HOW shame affects our bodies. I won't relist all the medical maladies I mentioned before, as I would rather focus on some physical manifestations that were affecting me of which I was not even aware. One was visible and another was audible. It was my wife, Kathy, who noticed these manifestations and was the only person who ever addressed them with me.

At first I thought she was clairvoyant or could read my mind. I knew that she had incredible spiritual discernment, hearing God when He speaks, but she always knew when I was on the phone with my mom. It was uncanny! Then she told me how she knew. Knowing about my childhood, Kathy tenderly shared what she witnessed when I answered our telephone.

"I can always tell it's your mother on the phone, because you pull your shoulders up, as if you are trying to hide." She then added, "Your entire posture changes."

Here I was, a grown man, living more than six hundred miles from my mother and yet my body would involuntarily take the posture of a scolded child. That same posture would manifest every time I was in the company of people around whom I felt "less than." Over the years Kathy lovingly reminded me that I belong and can put my shoulders back. Besides, she thinks I look sexier with good posture.

Another manifestation of shame was audible.

What did you say?" Kathy would ask.

"Huh. Oh nothing."

This odd and uncomfortable conversation took place between us For years. Again it was Kathy who noticed that which I was completely unaware of. Shame has an effect on our thoughts, beliefs, body, and actions. With Kathy's help I learned it also has a voice—a voice that sounded a lot like me.

What Kathy responded to were involuntary vocalizations, which were most often without words. They were more like grunts, sighs, or expressions of exasperation. She would become frustrated because I was clearly communicating something, but I would become embarrassed and immediately shut down the conversation by saying, "It's nothing." What was going on inside of me, however, was anything but nothing! I would emit these subtle vocal outbursts that I now refer to as "shame attacks." Shame often leads a person to ruminate about the past. Shame uses our internal conversations and self-criticisms and turns them into ruminations. There's a word for you: rumination.

It's a psychological term that means the following: "to chew the cut; chew again what has been chewed slightly and swallowed."[7] Rumination is similar to worry, except rumination focuses on bad feelings and experiences from the past, whereas worry is concerned with potential bad events in the future. Both rumination and worry are associated with anxiety and other negative emotional states. And just so we are clear, ruminating is a verb.

Believe it or not, there is even a medical condition called rumination syndrome, an eating disorder in which a person, usually an infant or young child, brings back up and re-chews partially digested food that has already been swallowed. In most cases, the re-chewed food is then swallowed again, but occasionally the child will spit it out. Gross! And yet some of us do this emotionally and mentally on a daily basis.

I compare ruminating to falling overboard from a boat (or voluntarily swimming) in the Great Barrier Reef with open sores and lacerations. Sooner or later you are bound to experience a shark attack. Similarly, when we voluntarily or involuntarily focus on our distresses, past sins, or mistakes, shame sniffs these gaping emotional wounds and prepares for a shame attack.

A shame attack can happen to me whether I'm having a good or bad day. It doesn't matter. As abruptly as falling overboard, all it takes is a thought, a smell, a word, or a person's name and the ruminations begin. I can ruminate about events that happened when I was five years old as easily as events that happened five minutes ago. It's not unusual for someone battling shame to leave a

---

7 *Webster's Collegiate Dictionary,* Third Edition of the Merriam Series, "Ruminate" (Springfield, MA: G. & C. Merriam Co., 1928).

room of friends, family, or co-workers and immediately begin self-criticizing for talking too much, not talking enough, being too funny, being too serious, being… whatever. Sound familiar? Shame will manifest in what we say to ourselves voluntarily and involuntarily.

Once a thought, smell, word, or name associated with a negative experience presents itself to me, I have to immediately battle it. In the past, these thoughts would make my back and neck grow hot and then break into a sweat. I would focus on everything I did wrong concerning an event and begin saying negative things to myself.

Eventually I would involuntarily grunt, sigh, or mutter something like, "You're such a loser" or "You idiot" or "I hate myself!" The most common was "What's wrong with you?" And if Kathy was within earshot, she would ask, "Did you say something?" With red-faced embarrassment I would lie and reply, "No."

It took many years and many attempts on her part to eventually break through. Part of the problem was I didn't know what was going on inside of me, and quite frankly I was embarrassed. Here I was suffering from emotional indigestion, burping out sounds and words that I couldn't control. It was enough to drive a person crazy… both of us.

One day she pressed the issue after one of my shame attacks and said, "Do you know who that sounded like?" And then she named a person. I was stunned. She accurately discerned the person I was ruminating about.

James gives wise counsel:

Therefore confess your sins [faults, offences] to each other and pray for each other so that you may be healed. The prayer of a righteous person is powerful and effective.
—James 5:16

By ruminating on the past, I would withdraw and begin mentally and emotionally isolating myself from family and friends, and particularly my wife. The cardinal rule for swimming is to never swim alone, yet I would be swimming in shark-infested waters, choosing to remain isolated and alone, even though Kathy was nearby with a life preserver. She never gave up.

Now when a shame attack comes—yes, I still have a tendency to fall overboard—and I vocalize with an "ugh" or a sigh, Kathy is quick to respond with "Are you okay?" or "What do you need?" or "I'm here if you need me." She's learned to recognize the sound of a shame attack and knows my tendency to swim alone.

Because Kathy is a good listener and rarely in fix-Steve mode, when I share with her what I am ruminating on, she sheds light on my dark thoughts. With her help, I walk out from darkness and toward God's marvelous light, where I can forgive myself, another person, or both.

If you currently experience, or have experienced, shame attacks like mine, I encourage you to have someone you trust to read this chapter. By doing so, you can bring this issue from darkness into the light. If they are reading this, they know that you trust them and are asking for their help. This help is not to find fault, fix you, or dispense Christianized sound bites, but to help you according to Paul's exhortation to the Galatians:

> *Carry one another's burdens and in this way you will fulfill the requirements of the law of Christ [that is, the law of Christian love]. For if anyone thinks he is something [special] when [in fact] he is nothing [special except in his own eyes], he deceives himself.*
>
> —Galatians 6:2–3, AMP

Dealing with an overwhelming shame attack is not fun or easy for either one of us, but together my wife and I fend off the sharks by openly addressing thoughts and old thought patterns that help me get out of shark-infested waters and back on dry land.

24

Shame in the Church

If you didn't know better, you might believe that the church was established for the purpose of modifying the behavior of sinners. From my experiences as a church member, and then pastor, I've come to realize that this impression is quite common among believers and non-believers alike. Story after story of a church hurt has been shared with me. Before continuing, I want to remind the reader that there are always two sides to every story.

> *In a lawsuit the first to speak seems right, until someone comes forward and cross-examines.*
>
> —Proverbs 18:17

I've seen occasions when the church was in the wrong. I've also witnessed people who believed the church wronged them and were actually the ones at fault. So I will do my best to offer both sides, as I'm not choosing sides, just pulling off a spiritual Band-Aid of sorts.

Since this chapter primarily focuses on the church and ministries, it has the potential to offend some people more than any other chapter. It's not my intent to bring reproach upon the church or ministry leaders; my desire is to address what I've seen and experienced as a systemic problem of shame in our churches and ministries of all denominations.

Since this is such a touchy issue, let's start with an old joke.

A passing merchant ship rescues a man who has been stranded on a deserted island for many years. The captain dispatches three crewmembers in a lifeboat to the island. Once ashore, the ecstatic castaway tells the crewmembers of his ten-year existence on the island. He shows them the fruit trees that were his only source of food and the freshwater stream among the palm trees. He shows them his grass-covered hut and then points to a similar structure several feet away and informs them that this is his church. They ask if there is anyone else on the island, because several hundred feet away is another grass-covered hut. He tells them that there has never been anyone else on the island. Confused, they ask him what the other hut is. He looks disdainfully down the beach and says, "Oh that… that's the church I *used* to attend."

The reason that joke gets a laugh every time I tell it in a church is because there is a ring of truth to it. The laugh is usually an uncomfortable one, however, because people on both sides of the issue can relate. The only time this doesn't get a laugh is when I tell it to people who have never attended church. They just look at me puzzled, still waiting for the punchline.

Similar to the man stranded on the island, I've heard story after story of people being wounded by pastors, churches, and ministries, and now have a list of churches they *used* to attend. It's to the point now that a lot of people expect to be hurt or wounded in church, which leads to Christians being guarded and ready to bolt at the drop of a hat. Instead of finding a church home, a lot of Christians settle for a church hotel.

In a church hotel, a Christian never needs to unpack their baggage. They just live out of their suitcases until it's time to check out and find another church hotel. Why? Because they may have learned from experience, and as much as I hate to finish this sentence, that church isn't always a safe place for sinners.

Before sharing some modern-day examples, it's important to know that religious shaming has been around since the "first couple." The Bible is full of stories that record religious leaders using shame as a form of control, but it's not just leaders who employ shame this way; shaming is common to even us commoners. Remember the story of Mary and Martha in Luke 10?

As Jesus and his disciples were on their way, he came to a village where a woman named Martha opened her home to him. She had a sister called Mary, who sat at the Lord's feet listening to what he said. But Martha was distracted by all the preparations that had to be made. She came to him and asked, "Lord, don't you care that my sister has left me to do the work by myself? Tell her to help me!"

"Martha, Martha," the Lord answered, "you are worried and upset about many things, but few things are needed—or indeed only one. Mary has chosen what is better, and it will not be taken away from her."

—Luke 10:38–42

On His way to Jerusalem, Jesus stops by to visit the home of dear friends who happen to be the sisters of another dear friend named Lazarus. The narrative never indicates whether Jesus asked for food or not, but that didn't stop Martha from getting right to work on some Rice Krispie® treats when Jesus and the twelve arrived at her doorstep. All would have been fine if Martha wanted to serve her quests out of devotion, but it appears it was more out of religious or cultural duty—and that's why I believe she became so irritated with Mary.

Unlike Martha, Mary's love language was probably not "acts of service." It seems that Mary's love language was most likely "quality time." So there sat Mary, at the feet of Jesus, surrounded by the twelve disciples, while Martha slaved away in the kitchen. To be fair, Mary should not have been the only woman in the company of men so maybe, culturally speaking, this is why Martha became so irritated. Nah… she was mad about something common to us all. She was mad that she was doing all the work while Mary sat and did nothing.

It's time to unleash some shame.

After having an inner dialogue with herself about how right she was and how Mary was wronging her, Martha barges into the room where Jesus is sitting and says, and I quote, *"Lord, don't you care that my sister has left me to do all the work by myself? Tell her to help me!"* (Luke 18:40)

Two things here should capture your attention.

First, you will notice that Martha doesn't ask a question as much as she tries to manipulate the situation by being passive aggressive. Martha isn't being direct with Mary, but uses an indirect approach to get Jesus involved. Martha could have quietly gone to Mary and whispered that she could use some help, but instead she calls out Jesus for not caring while publicly shaming her sister in front of all the other guests. Martha is so amped up that she even refers to Mary as "my sister" rather than by name. Martha's summation of the situation is that no one appreciates her, that Mary is lazy, and that Jesus doesn't even care.

Second, after Martha vents her frustration, she turns and says to Jesus, the King of Kings and Lord of Lords, *"Tell her to help me!"* Oh my! Martha just told the Person who created the heavens and the earth what to do! I wonder if at this point Peter was thinking, *Man, I've said a lot of misguided things, but I would never had said that!*

Jesus deals with the situation between Martha and Mary with fond affection and grace for both. He starts by saying, *"Martha, Martha."* You will find this same double salutation a few other times in the New Testament: "Saul, Saul," "Simon, Simon," and "Jerusalem, Jerusalem." I learned from a mentor, Jack Deere, that when Jesus uses this double salutation, it means two things: Jesus' heart is filled with affection for that person (or city), and there is a rebuke coming.

> *Martha, Martha… you are worried and upset about many things, but few things are need—or indeed only one. Mary has chosen what is better, and it will not be taken away from her.*
>
> —Luke 10:41–42

Even before Jesus addresses Martha, we see in the narrative the cause of Martha's angst:

> *She had a sister called Mary, who sat at the Lord's feet listening to what he said. But Martha was distracted by all the preparations that had to be made.*
>
> —Luke 10:39–40

Even when we church folk seem to have the best of intentions, when us serving Jesus seems more important than being with Him and we get distracted, we become very aware of what everyone else is doing—or in this case, what others are not doing! It's so easy in church to believe that what we are doing for the Lord—be it a mission trip, volunteering at a shelter, teaching Sunday School, or even preaching a message—is the most important thing, even more important than the Lord or those we are serving.

Jesus makes a simple statement that should reverberate in our very souls: *"Mary has chosen what is better, and it will not be taken away from her"* (Luke 10:42). What Mary chose and will not be taken is the peace that comes from abiding in the presence of Jesus. That's why Paul states in Philippians 4:8–9,

> *Finally, brothers and sisters, whatever is true, whatever is noble, whatever is right, whatever is pure, whatever is lovely, whatever is admirable—if anything is excellent or praiseworthy—think about such things. Whatever you have learned or received or heard from me, or seen in me—put it into practice. And the God of peace will be with you.*

When we feel worried and upset that others don't appreciate our service to God, it may just be an early warning that we are distracted from Him and focused on ourselves.

Several years ago, a mother and daughter met with me to see if the church at which I served would be a good place for the daughter, Allison, who hadn't felt welcome at their former church.

Allison's mom shared what led up to meeting with me. "Allison is twelve years old and she desperately wants friends. Unfortunately, she was awkward and acted out in ways to get attention. One Wednesday night after youth group, I was informed by the youth pastor and another concerned parent that unless I accompanied and sat with Allison, she was no longer welcome to attend the group."

As I listened further, it became clear to me that in order for Allison to attend her church's youth group, she had to behave. I asked the mom what Allison was doing that had caused the youth pastor to make this request. She looked over to Allison and asked her to tell me instead.

"Well," Allison said, "while we were all listening to the pastor's message, I was trying to make the kids around me laugh." Looking down at the floor, she added that her youth pastor stopped his message and walked over to where she was sitting and stared at her until everyone else was staring at her, too.

"If you don't love Jesus enough to listen to this, then why are you even here?" the pastor asked.

Ouch! We continued talking and I asked her if she liked her youth pastor. She said she loved him—that is, until he embarrassed (shamed) her. I know what it's like to teach a room full of teens and preteens. It's like trying to teach a penguin, a water buffalo, a spider monkey, and a mule all at the same time. It's not easy and can become quite frustrating to communicate to the variety of species in the room.

As Allison continued to share, I thought back to my early experiences in ministry. My back broke out into a sweat. I regrettably could recall times when I had done things similar to what her youth pastor had done.

When Allison finished speaking, I looked at her and asked if she would forgive me. With a puzzled expression, she said, "What for?"

I replied, "For thinking that my message was more important than the people I was sharing it with."

She looked at me even more puzzled. "But I've never heard you speak before."

What I said next made both Allison and her mom begin to cry. "I know that, Allison, but there are some students that I need to apologize to for shaming them when I was new to ministry. But since they aren't in the room with us, I want to ask for your forgiveness on their behalf. And at the same time, I invite you to forgive your youth pastor."

How I wish what that youth pastor had done was foreign to me and that I had never shamed a student. The truth was, I had. I could remember in vivid detail when I had shamed a student.

Some restless nights and many phone calls followed my meeting with Allison and her mom. As far back as I could remember, I contacted every kid I felt that I had shamed. Their responses were all lovingly positive, but mixed. Some couldn't remember the incident I was apologizing for, while some did remember... clearly.

In these phone conversations, I realized that some people are more or less prone to shame's impact. Some former students responded with, "Aw, Pastor Steve, I deserved that! You weren't being mean to me, I was being a punk and I owe you the apology." Others said, "Wow, I can't believe you are calling me. I remember that night like it was yesterday. I was so embarrassed when you glared at me while you were speaking. You didn't say anything, but the way you looked at me made me feel so ashamed."

Either way, I was convicted in my heart that I had wronged some former students and needed to apologize. Some students, even during the tender teenage years, had a healthy response to shame. Instead of making a home for shame in their heart, they assessed the situation and concluded, "Yeah, Pastor Steve is being a bit of a jerk, but hey, I should be showing him some respect."

Some students were not as able, during adolescence, to put shame in its place and so they allowed shame to move in and find a home in their hearts. "Why does Pastor Steve hate me? All I was doing was repeating what he said to the kid next to me, because he didn't hear him. Why does he hate me?"

Until I called, one particular student was convinced that I hated her because I'd glared at her during my message. My temptation was to deflect this and assume that this was one overly sensitive kid who needed to toughen up. Maybe she just needed to rub some dirt on the wound and get back in the game. That may work in baseball, but the church is not a place where we simply call balls and strikes, and after three strikes you're out. No, we are called to love the unlovely, clothe the naked, feed the hungry, and provide shelter in the midst of life's storms.

We are not called to change people's behavior, but to minister to them and invite them to have a change of heart. What often happens to Christian leaders in the church is that they forget what it was like to not know how to behave.

It's similar to my selective memory of what an angel I was growing up, while bringing discipline to my own children. I truly don't remember acting that way when I was a kid, but I can assure you that I did act that way. Just ask my brother and sister.

Likewise, we Christian leaders can develop selective memory when it comes to our early days in the faith. If we're not careful, we can fall prey to the notion that a church member's behavior is solely a reflection of our ministry, so we can impose strict regulations on church members and even stricter regulations on other leaders. What develops next is the expectation that members will adhere to legalistic rules so as to prove their Christian growth, all while affirming our effectiveness in ministry.

I've heard this scenario repeated ad nauseam in my office. It saddens me that this is so prevalent in the church, but as James says, *"My brothers and sister, this should not be"* (James 3:10).

So what has happened in our churches that makes this a common theme in so many lives? I don't have a theory or explanation, but I do have a thought.

I have witnessed, both as a staff and church member, the shame used to control and manipulate staff members, lay leaders, and entire congregations. When shame becomes systemic in church leadership, the collateral damage is incalculable. I shudder to think how many people have lost faith in God because of the way some churches treat their members. By the same token, I shudder to think of how many pastors and ministry leaders have abandoned their calling because of the shame they received from elders, deacons, board members, and congregations. Sadly, there is no hurt quite like a church hurt.[8]

---

8 Because of my love for the churches and ministry staffs in which I have served over the last many years, I've included a bonus chapter at the back of this book. I used the father and his sons, found in Luke 15, as a way to describe the different types of leadership I have witnessed in the church.

25

Flipping Tables

THIS IS GOING TO BE SHORT AND SWEET. WELL, AT LEAST SHORT.

One of Jesus' most memorable ministry moments was when He went flipping over tables in the synagogue. What I find interesting is that none of the twelve disciples or the Apostle Paul ever did that. It's my belief that flipping tables is reserved for God's Son, and not for the rest of us. My belief is that since only Jesus led a sinless life and had pure and unmixed zeal for His Father's house, He and He alone could, with a pure heart, be that disruptive.

Unfortunately, I've known some leaders who gleefully take to table-flipping when correction or rebukes become necessary. A gleam comes to their eyes and they seem to salivate in preparation. In his letters to a young and immature pastor named Timothy, the Apostle Paul addresses the way we are to pastor, teach, correct, and in some cases bring rebuke. And nowhere is table-flipping mentioned.

In the early days of Paul's ministry, he could have been considered a table-flipper, as recorded in Acts 15. Paul had no time or patience for Mark, also referred to as John Mark, who had deserted their missionary team when they were in Pamphylia. Paul was so quick on the draw to drop John Mark from the team that it caused a fight between himself and Barnabas. It is important here to remember that it was Barnabas who first accepted and mentored Saul, the guy who was previously persecuting and killing Christians before being renamed Paul.

These two had such a sharp disagreement—which is Holy Spirit lingo for "they had a red-faced, spitting-mad argument"—that they had to part ways. Paul chose Silas as a travel companion and Barnabas took what was left of Mark. What I mean by "what was left" is that I'm fairly certain John Mark was dealing with not only the shame of deserting the team in Pamphylia and Paul's verbal dressing down, but also for having been the cause of the fight between Paul and Barnabas.

To top it off, he might have felt responsible for Barnabas leaving the ministry which Barnabas had invited Paul to join in the first place.

It's interesting to note that we never hear about Barnabas after this, except we do see the results of his ministry. His ministry was not to a country, a city, or a people group. It was to one person: Mark.

Let me backtrack for just a moment. I need to reintroduce Barnabas. Long before his well-known fight with Paul, Barnabas had a much different reputation. His real name was Joseph and he was a Levite. Barnabas was a nickname (the good kind) that meant "son of prophecy" or "son of encouragement" and he was known for his generosity according to Acts 4

Joseph—I mean, Barnabas—was also known for his wisdom as noted in Acts 11. There was a new move of God happening in Antioch and questions arose of its validity. So among all the apostles, including James the younger brother of Jesus, Barnabas was chosen to check things out and report back to the counsel in Jerusalem.

With that background information, we can deduce that Barnabas, a man known for his patience, generosity, and wisdom, chose Mark not because he was also a distant cousin, but because of Barnabas' character.

Now, back to where we left off. I mentioned that we don't hear about Barnabas after the brouhaha with Paul, but we do hear about Mark. Paul references him in Colossians 4 as someone to welcome even though the Colossians had heard about Mark. And guess whom they heard it from? Yup, the Apostle Paul himself. We again hear about Mark from Paul, who writes from prison in his second letter to Timothy, instructing the young pastor, *"Get Mark and bring him with you, because he is helpful to me in my ministry"* (2 Timothy 4:11).

The last time we hear about Mark is from the Apostle Peter, who refers to the one-time deserter of missionary teams as his son. History records that Mark was instrumental in the church being planted in Cyprus.

So what have we learned here concerning flipping tables? We'll let Paul answer that in his own words:

In the presence of God and of Christ Jesus, who will judge the living and the dead, and in view of his appearing and his kingdom, I give you this charge: Preach the word; be prepared in season and out of season; correct, rebuke and encourage— with great patience and careful instruction.

—2 Timothy 4:1–2

It's the phrase *"with great patience and careful instruction"* that captures my heart and reminds me that flipping tables is way above my paygrade... and yours, too.

26.

Baby Food

IN MY EFFORT TO DISCIPLE AND MENTOR OTHERS IN MY EARLY DAYS OF MINISTRY, I DIDN'T do too well adhering to Paul's advice to Timothy. Sure, I was very careful with instruction, most times, but the great patience part? Not so much. Notice, too, that the word "great" precedes the word patience. Paul is unambiguous and emphatic about this, so if you'll indulge me, I will paraphrase what he says in 2 Timothy 3:

> *Okay, listen up, Timmy. If you really are called to be a pastor, you need to get this settled in your heart. Sheep wander, sheep can be slow, and sometimes sheep will bite. After all my years of doing ministry, I've learned a thing or two from my friend Barnabas. If you are going to be effective in the teaching and mentoring areas of ministry, you will really need to study and know your stuff. And, just as importantly, you will need to dig deep and use every ounce of patience the Holy Spirit has worked in you. Trust me!*

If pastors, priests, ministers, and reverends are simply called to behavior modification, then flipping tables seems like a strategy we could easily employ. But if we are called to introduce people to Jesus, we need to leave the table-flipping to Him.

While feeding my grandson Jude (a.k.a. my little "love nugget") one day, this advice from Paul really hit home. If you've ever had the joy of spoon-feeding a baby, then you know well how time-consuming it can be. One spoonful of sweet potatoes can take several attempts before it's completely swallowed. You have to reintroduce the same spoonful again and again until they're ready for the second spoonful.

In their attempt to swallow, which includes the use of their tongue, a baby will unintentionally push the sweet potatoes out of their mouth as they try to figure out how their tongue is supposed to work. You then spend some time trying to catch what's on their chin with the spoon and try putting it in their mouth again. After several attempts, with the same initial spoonful, most of what you intended is finally in their tummy. Then and only then, you attempt spoonful number two.

Sure, spoon-feeding a baby can try your patience, yet at the same time, it's one of life's sweetest adventures, especially if that baby is your first grandchild. How shaming would it be for me to get frustrated and angry with Jude and flip over the tray on his highchair for not immediately knowing how the stick in Grandpa's hand has anything to do with eating? He might wonder why his grandpa is getting so mad at him, or wondering, *What's wrong with that bottle they used to give me? I can work that bottle thing all by myself, and then Grandpa won't be mad at me.*

But it's vitally important for Jude to learn to eat mashed-up baby food, because soon he will not be able to survive solely on milk. And he can't just rely on sweet potatoes either. As he grows, he will need to eat solid foods to sustain his life. So it is as vitally important for his grandpa to feed him as it is for him to learn how his tongue works and that Grandpa is in no rush to force him to gum a steak.

So with joy and a sense of wonder, I enjoy spoon-feeding my grandson, just as I did when his daddy and his aunt were babies. The little love nugget is learning about all kinds of tastes and textures while he learns to eat from a spoon. As of this writing, he's just about ready to take the spoon and feed himself, which was the plan all along.

Likewise as teachers, pastors, mentors, and parents, we should heed Paul's admonishment to carefully instruct with great patience, so that those we feed can *"[t]aste and see that the Lord is good"* (Psalm 34:8). And without using teaching methods that include shame, we instill in them the ability and personal desire to feed themselves on His Word so that the church can avoid raising a generation of immature believers, who are mentioned in Hebrews:

> *In fact, though by this time you ought to be teachers, you need someone to teach you the elementary truths of God's word all over again. You need milk, not solid food!*
> —Hebrews 5:12

So again, teachers and leaders take heed: we can unintentionally shame those we are supposed to teach and lead by force-feeding or becoming impatient with those who are precious in His sight… and that includes grownups, too.

27.

Lack of Faith Shame

Because you have so little faith. Truly I tell you, if you have faith as small as a mustard seed, you can say to this mountain, "Move from here to there,"' and it will move.

—Matthew 17:20

"You know, Steve, ten years ago I thought the hardest thing I would ever do was have to tell my nine-year-old son that his mommy was dying of cancer. Boy was I ever wrong."

My friend's words hung thick in the air as we stood next to my car parked in the street in front of his house. I stood there speechless, as I had no words with which to respond, trying to take in everything I had just witnessed in the last forty-five minutes. He didn't say anything else and neither did I. We just stood there next to my car, both wishing and praying that maybe it was all a dream.

Several months earlier, my friend's teenage son had been diagnosed with bone cancer, and after multiple surgeries, chemotherapy, and radiation treatments the cancer spread to his lungs. It soon became evident that without miraculous intervention, cancer would take his son's life. I was privileged to walk this journey with father and son, as a pastor at their church—but beyond the pastor/member relationship, we were friends.

On this day, I had just witnessed one of the most beautifully awful moments I've ever experienced. I watched a father who dearly loved his son, and only child, deliver news that no parent should ever have to give. He asked a few weeks earlier if I would be present when he had to break the news to his son. Even as I assured him that I would be there, I was praying for a miracle that would negate me having to be present.

Shameless

As I said before, it was a beautifully awful experience to witness. Beautiful in how this father loved his son and how this son loved his father. How lovely was the trust this son had in his father, as this father delivered a devastatingly emotional blow to his son. I sat there frozen and found it difficult to breathe as the father spoke.

"Son, I have something to share with you and I asked Steve to be here while I tell you," he began. His son knew that it wasn't going to be good news, not only because of his father's tone, but that I was also there. "Son, the doctors have done all that they can do, and at this point they don't want to subject you to any more surgeries. They also don't recommend any further chemo or radiation treatments. So we are at the place where unless Jesus does a miracle, you will be meeting Him face to face fairly soon."

I think I was still holding my breath when my friend looked inquisitively at me. I nodded, affirming that he was doing wonderfully and to keep going. He asked his son if he had any questions, and as you would expect, he did have some questions. My friend was amazing, as he lovingly answered every question that his son had. Occasionally my friend would look over at me with the same inquisitive look, and I would again nod to affirm that he was doing marvelously. His son had a couple of questions for me that I did my best to answer. We prayed together, and before leaving I kissed his chemo-induced bald head.

My friend walked outside with me, and as soon as the front door was shut behind us, he whacked me on the arm and said, "Why didn't you say anything?"

Rubbing my arm, I replied, "I didn't know you wanted me to!"

"Why the heck did you think I kept looking over at you?" he shot back.

"I thought you were just looking at me to see if I thought you were doing okay! And you were *amazing!*"

It was as if a pressure valve opened up and we simultaneously chuckled at our lack of nonverbal communication skills.

"Another reason I didn't say anything was because I was witnessing one of the most holy and beautiful things I've ever seen," I said as we walked to the car. "In fact, I don't think I breathed for the first five minutes."

My friend didn't say anything for the rest of the walk.

When I unlocked the car doors, he finally spoke again. It's a sentence forever burned into my soul.

"You know, Steve, ten years ago I thought the hardest thing I would ever do was have to tell my nine-year-old son that his mommy was dying of cancer. Boy was I ever wrong."

This same father, who had just delivered the horrible news to his son, had ten years earlier, almost to the day, delivered similarly devastating news that his mommy was dying of brain cancer. Like I said before, the air was thick.

My friend walked back into his house as I sat in my car gathering my thoughts. Another church member then arrived at the house to visit and encourage the family. I was grateful for the reinforcements and really liked this person. But the joy and relief was shattered when this well-meaning and truly godly person began questioning me, asking if my friend, as the spiritual priest of his household, had taken authority over the devil and claimed healing for his son. It was like a punch in the gut.

Shame likes to ride on the shoulders of well-meaning Christians, who in their zeal for miracles and healing can oftentimes not be as discerning as they are zealous.

They suggest that if only we had more faith, all of our dreams would come true and the primrose path would be ours to enjoy for the rest of our lives. As I stated earlier, I believe that God heals and still does miracles, but as He wills. When the Pharisees demanded a sign or miracle, Jesus gently responded, *"Very truly I tell you, the Son can do nothing by himself; he can do only what he sees his Father doing, because whatever the Father does the Son also does"* (John 5:19).

Far too often, well-meaning believers can get focused on a particular doctrine, teaching, or manifestation of spiritual gifts and forsake love, discernment, and listening for God's voice.

It felt like this other brother was approaching the situation with legalism and judgment more than love and concern. He was judging whether my friend had enough faith instead of aching for him. I was about to verbally unload on him when I recalled a similar desire to rip someone's head off in Jesus' name.

About an hour before I was to speak at a Christian music festival, I decided to stick my backstage pass in my pocket and stroll around and mingle with the audience. Most of the audience had never heard of me, so it was easy to be anonymous once I hid the backstage pass. Soon two young men who looked like a cover photo for a church bulletin approached and warmly greeted me. After a few pleasantries were exchanged, one of them pointed to the plastic bottle I was carrying and asked what I was drinking. I replied that it was Gatorade when suddenly he took it from my hand, smelled the contents, and handed it back to me.

I was so stunned and surprised at this that I stood frozen, transfixed by their chutzpa and audacity.

Did they just sniff my drink to see if I was drinking alcohol? Surely not, I thought.

Surely yes, for that's exactly what they were doing. I asked them if they were with a group and they said the name of a church in the area. They had come to the Christian music festival to minister to people. I was about to take offense when I remembered that I needed to head backstage because I had to speak in a few minutes.

On the way to the backstage area, I kept going over in my head what a couple of jerks they were. I couldn't wait to go onstage and then call out to them, saying, "Hey you two jerks over there, you remember me?" Had those guys even prayed about confronting me or was it my appearance (torn jeans, ponytail, untucked shirt) that caused them to approach me?

The two young men sized me up, and in their view and maybe experience, I looked like a guy who needed to get saved. My offended response was to size them up as arrogant little legalists who needed to be publicly humiliated from stage.

Thank the Lord God Almighty, the walk to the backstage area was long enough for me to pray, choose to overlook the offense, forgive them, and also ask for forgiveness for my own bitter judgments.

When we choose to view others with our natural eyes instead of our spiritual eyes, we open up a spiritual can of worms. Paul addresses this in his first letter to the church at Corinth:

> *So from now on we regard no one from a human point of view [according to worldly standards and values]. Though we have known Christ from a human point of view, now we no longer know Him in this way. Therefore if anyone is in Christ [that is, grafted in, joined to Him by faith in Him as Savior], he is a new creature [reborn and renewed by the Holy Spirit]; the old things [the previous moral and spiritual condition] have passed away. Behold, new things have come [because spiritual awakening brings a new life].*
>
> —2 Corinthians 5:16–17, AMP

Now back to my friend's front yard and the well-meaning church member. He was looking solely through the lens of his healing theology; he assumed that if only my friend had enough faith, he would take a stand as the priest and head of his household that his son would be cancer-free. Through the lens of my "what the hell are you doing?" emotional turmoil, I assumed this brother needed a kick in the pants. What *I* needed was another long walk to the backstage area.

As easily as shame came riding in on this person's shoulders to potentially shame my friend for lacking faith or not being the priest of his household, shame was potentially ready to take a ride on my shoulders and shame the person who truly meant well. What a mess!

Fortunately, my friend was already inside, and I had the music festival experience under my belt, so I thanked the church member for coming, but I also asked them to let a father be alone with his son. I didn't try to correct them or teach them about God's sovereignty; we simply joined hands and prayed there in the street that the Lord of heaven would provide my friend with peace and the healing of His choosing for his son.

A few weeks later, the son left his earthly body and did meet Jesus face to face. Since then, my friend became my right-hand man while I was the missions pastor at a church in northern Georgia. He now leads mission trips, and he and his wife (who, in the words of their son, was "the best stepmom a boy could have") are currently in the process of adopting four girls from Haiti. My friend was able to release his son into the hands of his Creator and not suffer the effects of shame that sometimes come from well-meaning Christians.

My friend will tell you that God answers prayers three ways: yes, not yet, and no. It's when He answers no that we need to resist the shame that tells us we didn't believe or have enough faith and, like Habakkuk, declare:

Though the fig tree does not bud and there are no grapes on the vines, though the olive crop fails and the fields produce no food, though there are no sheep in the pen and no cattle in the stalls, yet I will rejoice in the Lord, I will be joyful in God my Savior. The Sovereign Lord is my strength; he makes my feet like the feet of a deer, he enables me to tread on the heights.

—Habakkuk 3:17–19

Oh, and by the way, the story within the story of this chapter is in no ways a commentary on drinking. So there.

28

The Shame of Blessings

I'VE BEEN BLESSED AND PRIVILEGED TO BE ON MORE SHORT-TERM MISSION TRIPS THAN I can count. If I took the time, I could probably add them up, but a few years ago I stopped keeping track because it became a not-so-subtle place for pride to find a home in me. I do treasure the countries, people, and adventures that I've encountered as well as the missionaries whom I've served with. I am grateful. I used to feel guilty.

There are few things that you can count on during a short-term mission trip. The first is that you can't count on anything. If you have a plan, a schedule, or a timetable that you are going to adhere to, what you really have is a binder full of useless paper and an opportunity to have your patience tested. Trust me.

Another thing is culture shock... when you return home. It's usually after someone's first mission trip to an impoverished area or country that I hear a person say that they feel so guilty about all they have and all their blessings. That statement may sound like the trip gave them a new worldview, but it doesn't equate to a biblical worldview. There is nothing redemptive about feeling guilty or ashamed for your blessings, as that only paralyzes you. Being grateful can be a powerfully redemptive force in our lives. Gratitude is a force that can compel and empower us to continue to do good works in the world.

How crazy is it that our blessings or the good things in our lives can shame some of us? We can feel shame when we are poor and shame when we are rich. Ahhh! Okay, got that out of my system. Here's the deal... if you are blessed, be grateful, not guilty. It's my belief that much of Hollywood's misguided advocacy is due to some feelings of guilt for being wealthy and famous, which tends to make for a relatively easy life. Think about it. What in fact do the Kardashians really do? They are famous for being famous, right?

Conversely, if you look at the Robertson families from A&E's popular series *Duck Dynasty*, you see families who are grateful for and handle their blessings well. First and foremost, they had a successful business (Duck Commander) and were compensated for providing goods and services. Their notoriety first came as a result of their business savvy and success, which made them interesting to the folks at A&E. Only then did they become celebrities, and their newfound celebrity status didn't seem to change them very much. They still hold to their Christian faith and values and are still as generous, if not more so, than they were before. So why am I taking time to write about those bearded boys? It's because I know people who, like the Robertson families, are blessed but have dealt with guilt-infused shame for being blessed. It typically manifests on mission trips.

Whenever I've led mission trips, it's been my experience that some who participate can become forlorn and guilt-ridden because of what they have compared to what little those they are serving have. It happens almost every time. Actually, it's happened every time, at least on the trips I've been a part of. Once the trip is over, participants will return to their normal lives and battle feelings of guilt. But guilt is not redemptive or empowering. Guilt is shaming, paralyzing, and also fleeting.

After a few weeks back home, those strong feelings of guilt tend to fade as the maintenance of normal life returns. Regularly participants that made decisions or vows on the mission field based upon guilt will rethink these decisions and vows and either forget or dismiss them. It's similar to when someone decides to sponsor a child at a concert, conference, or event because of guilt. Working as a spokesperson/advocate for child sponsorship ministries and organizations, I know firsthand that upwards of fifty percent of those who agree to sponsor a child at an event do not fulfill their sponsorship once they get home. Sadly, this costs these organizations and ministries more time and money. You see, guilt does not usually produce much heart change. Gratitude, however, can change a heart forever. And true gratitude is empowering and never fleeting.

When we resist thoughts of guilt for our blessings, which can lead to shame, and exchange them for thoughts of gratitude and grace, we can accept them and make better decisions because of our blessings. Gratitude brings a healthy perspective that allows us to become even more aware that our blessings come from God who has freely blessed us.

And my God will meet all your needs according to the riches of his glory in Christ Jesus.

—Philippians 4:19

126

All this is from God, who reconciled us to himself through Christ and gave us the ministry of reconciliation…

—2 Corinthians 5:18

His divine power has given us everything we need for a godly life through our knowledge of him who called us by his own glory and goodness.

—2 Peter 1:3

As gratitude allows us to put blessings in perspective, we begin to realize that when we are blessed, we are to bless others.

Command those who are rich in this present world not to be arrogant nor to put their hope in wealth, which is so uncertain, but to put their hope in God, who richly provides us with everything for our enjoyment.

—1 Timothy 6:17

As you go, proclaim this message: "The kingdom of heaven has come near." Heal the sick, raise the dead, cleanse those who have leprosy, drive out demons. Freely you have received; freely give.

—Matthew 10:7–8

Here's a little saying I came up with when doing short-term mission training: "Guilt will freeze you up, while gratitude will free you up."

As my friend Will Davis says, "If you have more than enough and you know someone who has less than enough, then it's up to you to move toward enough first so that others can move toward enough with your help through generosity." It's a simple thought, but it works!

So if you are blessed, be grateful, not guilty. Perhaps you need to fulfill the promise you made to sponsor a child, maybe go on another mission trip, but now being set free from the guilty feelings that shame would otherwise bind you with, you are free to go forth and be a blessing!

29.

The Orphan Spirit

MANY WHO SUFFER SHAME HAVE A TENDENCY TO THINK AND BEHAVE LIKE AN ORPHAN. It's as if they've developed an orphan spirit, which causes them to focus on what they don't have. They define themselves by the lack in their lives, especially when it comes to their needs when they were growing up.

Orphaned thinking, brought on by shame, will often make people desire, pursue, and chase after things that they don't need. They will commonly manifest this by purchasing clothing or shoes they'll never wear and collecting things like trinkets, collectables or even Happy Meal® toys to fill a void. This type of thinking is very common among those who suffer from the psychological disorder of hoarding. Many hoarders collect and retain not only trinkets and collectables, but they also the sorts of things healthy people would put in a trashcan. There are reality TV shows galore based on hoarders. Hoarders, who have been exposed by family members in hopes that a TV show might fix the problem, are filmed in their homes, where mounds of junk surround them. The TV producers send a cleanup crew and either a psychiatrist, psychologist, or therapist to assist in the effort.

If you have ever watched an episode of a show like this, you've probably wondered if it's all scripted because of the insanity of the hoarder. Sadly, there is no script. These are real-life situations, documented on film for our culture's viewing pleasure. These people are most likely emotionally crippled by the power of shame, and the goal is to get the house cleaned up and for the hoarder to stop hoarding. It's frustrating, though, because I've yet to hear of an episode in which the issue of shame gets addressed. Collecting, hoarding or even a clean house will never fill the void created by shame; only the redemptive love of God through Jesus Christ can fill the emptiness.

Sons and daughters, on the other hand, don't focus on what they *don't* have, but are grateful for what they *do* have. When asked how they are doing, they respond with "Better than I deserve," as coined by Dave Ramsey. Sons and daughters don't just reply with clichés; they really believe that life (the good along with the bad) is a gift from God. They've learned to thank God in all situations. Like the Apostle Paul, they've learned to be content in all situations. Yet, all the while, our culture battles against, and even undermines, a grateful attitude.

Think about the words and phrases advertisers use to create a sense of need in us: "New and improved," "For a limited time only," "Latest version," and "iPhone® 22." Okay, there isn't an iPhone® 22... yet. But you see what I mean?

Sons and daughters see a commercial about the latest, newest, and improved version of whatever they have and think, *My version still works, and it's paid for.* An orphan tends to think, *Everyone else is getting the new version, so my current version must be a piece of junk. I need that new version to be just as current and measure up to everyone else.* Orphans are consumed with what everyone else has and strive to measure up to some preconceived standard that shame has instituted.

Sons and daughters are content, knowing that they already measure up, because they are loved. They are not consumed with what others think of them or whether others have what they don't have. They are comforted and content with being who they are and grateful for what they already have.

Do you think, believe, or behave like an orphan? Do you focus or ruminate on what you don't have? Do you compulsively collect things? Do you hoard? Are you counting down the time before the next Apple keynote address? If so, there is hope, and you have an invitation to think, believe, and behave as a son or daughter.

Listen to what Jesus says to His disciples, in probably their most fearful and uncertain hour—the night He was arrested and taken from them.

And I will ask the Father, and He will give you another Helper (Comforter, Advocate, Intercessor—Counselor, Strengthener, Standby), to be with you forever... I will not leave you as orphans [comfortless, bereaved, and helpless]; I will come [back] to you.

—John 14:16, 18, AMP

I have told you these things, so that in Me you may have [perfect] peace. In the world you have tribulation and distress and suffering, but be courageous [be confident, be undaunted, be filled with joy]; I have overcome the world." [My conquest is accomplished, My victory abiding.]

—John 16:33, AMP

In the Old Testament, the Lord speaks these words to the prophet Isaiah:

Do not be afraid; you will not be put to shame. Do not fear disgrace; you will not be humiliated. You will forget the shame of your youth and remember no more the reproach of your widowhood.

—Isaiah 54:4

And our beloved brother, the Apostle Paul, who had lots of reasons to allow his past sins to shame him into thinking his sins were such that he could never be welcomed as a son in God's kingdom, writes:

Even though I was once a blasphemer and a persecutor and a violent man, I was shown mercy because I acted in ignorance and unbelief. The grace of our Lord was poured out on me abundantly, along with the faith and love that are in Christ Jesus. Here is a trustworthy saying that deserves full acceptance: Christ Jesus came into the world to save sinners—of whom I am the worst. But for that very reason I was shown mercy so that in me, the worst of sinners, Christ Jesus might display his immense patience as an example for those who would believe in him and receive eternal life. Now to the King eternal, immortal, invisible, the only God, be honor and glory for ever and ever. Amen.

—1 Timothy 1:13–17

And because of God's loving grace, Paul's transformation from his past sins, and the shame that accompanied it, inspired him to write:

For I am not ashamed of the gospel, because it is the power of God that brings salvation to everyone who believes: first to the Jew, then to the Gentile.

—Romans 1:16

You can be set free from an orphan mentality. You can stop compulsively collecting, and you can stop hoarding, because you can do all things through Jesus Christ who strengthens you. I invite you to put this book down for a few minutes (remember where you put it) to pause and digest some of what I shared in this chapter. You might think it was silly to include Happy Meal® toys in my list of collectibles, and well you should, but I have an attic filled with boxes of them. You might think I'm assuming that all hoarders suffer with shame. You're right again… partly. I believe that shame plays some role in the hoarding disorder.

Lastly, you might think I believe that Jesus is the answer. And this time you are one hundred percent correct.

I believe that Jesus is the answer to the ache and pain of all emotional suffering. I believe with all that is within me, but if you don't believe that Jesus is the answer, *that's okay*. That's the reason I'd like for you to put this book down for those few minutes I mentioned to risk saying a prayer. Heck, you don't even have to call it a prayer… you can simply talk and say, "Jesus, if You are real and are really listening to me and really do love and really do care for me, *help!* I need a life preserver!"

If you're still holding this book, or have picked it back up, this is my prayer for you:

Heavenly Father, I know that you hear me. You always hear me when I pray, so on behalf of the one who is reading this, I ask for Your comfort, strength, and encouragement to come forth. I pray that You would reveal Yourself and Your compassion for this dear one through unexpected blessings, divinely timed encounters, and conversations. I also pray for those who already know You as Lord and Savior, as well as those who have yet to come to trust You by faith, to be released from their spiritual and emotional orphanage. I ask that You would expose and shed light on the areas in their past that led to and reinforced their orphaned thinking and behavior, and set them on their journey to wholeness. I ask this in the name of Jesus. Amen.

30.

The Shame Pendulum

As I was nearing the end of writing this book, something happened that made me include this chapter, which was initially meant as a message for a camp I was speaking at. I almost didn't include this, but I could not shake its significance. The shame pendulum is how the church seemingly responds to *everything*.

It wasn't that long ago that going to a pool hall, movie theater, drinking a beer or glass of wine, or (Lord forbid) dancing could jeopardize a person's salvation. I harken back to when I first started doing comedy in churches. The scrutiny was intense. These days, Christian comics can say things that I was run out of churches for. I also remember being the opening act for Christian bands when certain churches would not allow drums in their buildings. We even had picketers at some shows. We've come a long way, baby, but the pendulum is still swinging in other ways.

As I mentioned earlier, while working on the rewrites for this book, within a span of a few days, I received several invitations via texts, emails, and phone calls to attend a gathering of believers from the surrounding counties who come and pray together and share testimonies of God's amazing power and grace. The first few invites listed the basics—day, time, and place. I was excited to hear about this gathering and was looking forward to attending when I was in town. The next few invites, however, gave me pause.

Something that was of utmost importance to some of my inviters was that, at this gathering, no pastors were allowed to speak. My first thought was that this was a loving gesture toward pastors, so they would be able to attend and not feel pressured to have to prepare a message. Truth be told, pastors love to talk at events like this one.

But after encountering a friend at Starbucks, I soon discovered that the reason for not allowing pastors to speak was not as loving as I first thought. This friend had attended the gathering a few times and loved it. It sounded like a great time of ministry and fellowship, and the experience was all upbeat and encouraging.

All of a sudden, his facial expression and countenance changed. His smile morphed into what I could best describe as a sneer.

"And the best part is that no pastors ever get to speak!" he said.

How ironic, I thought, not just because of his words, but how his demeanor changed when he said, "And the best part is..." In fact, his entire mood changed, and became negative about almost everything we talked about after that.

Want to know what the ironic part is? This friend is all about grace, grace, and even more grace! In fact, his position on grace makes it hard for him to call sin "sin." What could have caused this hyper-grace guy to become so harsh? I'll give you three guesses and the first two don't count. I almost asked him if a pastor had hurt him, but that was obvious and I didn't have the time to have that level of conversation with him. We parted cordially, and I headed for my car.

Before driving away, I sat there for a moment, observing my friend through the big windows. He seemed to recover his happier mood as he sat in one of the leather chairs to drink his coffee. I kept looking at him and heard his words again: "And the best part is that no pastors ever get to speak." So the best part of this gathering wasn't the prayer, fellowship, or ministry; it was that no pastors were allowed to speak.

Before backing out of the parking space I offered up a quick prayer: "Dear Lord, please release my friend from whatever happened to him that makes him dislike pastors so much."

I can relate. I've been a pastor and have been pastored. I know both sides of the coin. I've been hurt by pastors, and I am sad to say that as a pastor I've hurt others. Thank God for His merciful grace and His Spirit, who prompts us when we need to ask for or offer forgiveness. What was happening in my friend happens in so many others every day. A pastor hurt him, so he was going to push the pendulum back the other way, as hard as he could. While sneering, with vengeful joy he shared the part about no pastors speaking. If a pastor had hurt him, then by golly, he was going to hurt them right back... the whole lot of them. What a thrill it must have been for him to know that it wasn't just one pastor who wasn't allowed to speak at this event... no pastors were allowed to speak, not even one, ever!

So how does this make the pastors who attend this gathering feel? I wonder if the no-pastors-can-speak rule picks at a wound they received from an elder, deacon, or church member. What if there are pastors in attendance who have been shamed by the very people they are called to serve and now attend a gathering where at least some of the leaders are anti-pastor? Here's another question: what if God wants to use a pastor in this environment?

The irony is that because someone was wounded by legalism, the solution was to answer legalism with a different expression of legalism. And that is where we see the pendulum swing back the other way.

Not surprisingly, there are many more good pastors than there are bad pastors. On the one hand, some may read that and wonder how dare I say there are bad pastors, while on the other hand some may emphatically state just the opposite and claim that there are no good pastors. How you reacted to my statement has more to do with your (or another's) experience with pastors rather than statistics or even the truth. The truth is, there are good pastors and there are bad pastors. There are also good teachers and bad teachers, good lawyers and bad lawyers... I don't need to keep going, right? You get the gist?

One doctrine of Christian faith is to respect authority and honor leaders, and some Christian leaders have covered up sins using this part of the Gospel as a cloak of infallibility and invincibility when dealing with their own shortcomings. I've heard countless stories of people who were under authoritarian leaders and then, after leaving that church, were hyperaware and hypersensitive to any message that had the word "authority" in it. This would cause them to start seeking yet another church, or simply not attend one at all.

Sadly, some pastors and ministry leaders have used manipulation and even intimidation on their members, causing them to believe that any questions concerning their behavior or their ministry is an attack from the enemy and must be dealt with. What often happens is that pastors will preach about Jezebel, the rebellion of the Israelites, or the persecution of the disciples when they feel they are being attacked.

Ironically, this is when those same pastors and ministry leaders should be reading the passages about Samuel confronting King Saul, Paul confronting Peter, or John getting ready to deal with Diotrephes. Leaders should read these, and many other Bible stories like them, when they feel that their authority or leadership is being questioned. It's good for pastors to remember that David didn't take the throne by force, nor did he defend it when his own son sought to take from him. Jesus offered no defense to His accusers. Paul apologized to the high priest when he realized his arrogance, and so on.

What is so sad to me is that you rarely, if ever, hear about the good pastors on the local news, because they aren't good news stories (pun intended). It's only when pastors behave badly that they are "good" news stories. In my experience, the very best pastors are ones most people have never heard of. Quietly, they devote themselves to ministering to those entrusted to them, and like I said before, it's not a good news story for the media.

Because of the media coverage of pastors behaving badly, it could appear that they are the norm rather than the exception, and that all pastors are money- and power-hungry charlatans. Well, if you had never attended a church or had a bad experience with a pastor, you might have the impression that all pastors are bad.

Likewise, the very same news story might leave others shocked and appalled. Why? Because in their view, every pastor they've ever known was wonderful. We all view things through the lens of our experience.

If we've been hurt by a church, we may give it a try by attending another church, but our bags are still packed, and now locked, just in case there is a need for a quick getaway. This defensive posture is one of the very reasons why pastors and church leaders get wounded. In their attempt to minister to the wounded person, they themselves are wounded and can begin to believe that all church members are bad. And so the pendulum continues to swing back and forth, from side to side, knocking down everyone in its path.

Is there a pastor or ministry leader who came to mind while you read this? Maybe you are a pastor or ministry leader and you thought of a church member or coworker in ministry. To deal with the pendulum, you most likely need to offer forgiveness to someone else and ask for forgiveness yourself.

Shame would love for us to keep riding the pendulum between feeling ashamed that we can't consistently obey all of God's commands and not having enough grace for other people. That broad sweeping pendulum never allows us to rest in a healthy place of divine tension—that is, being a sinner saved by grace (not following rules) while offering grace to other sinners (including ourselves) who just might happen to be pastors. And after all, the Bible is true no matter who quotes it.

Just prior to submitting this for print, I received word that a friend of mine, who is a pastor, was invited to speak at the event I have been writing about. I was so overjoyed to hear that he spoke and that the pendulum is starting to swing back. I do hope and pray that it comes to rest in the middle, otherwise it will be only pastors speaking. Isn't that what Sundays are for?

31.

Pause Button

For my friend, Jason, the best bass player I know.

I was in a department store recently and witnessed something that was so awkward and uncomfortable that I literally pressed myself into one of those circular clothing racks. Once safely surrounded by Mr. Ralph Lauren's creations, I continued to watch this slow-motion train wreck. It involved an irate customer and a shell-shocked salesclerk. I thought to myself, *Doesn't that lady realize how she's acting? Is she really throwing a temper-tantrum right here, in front of all these people?*

I answered my own questions: "I don't think so" and "Yes."

She seemed completely detached from her actions as she did an amazing interpretation of a two-year-old demanding another cupcake, unconcerned that people were watching. Finally she shrieked a few choice words, pushed items that were on the sales counter to the floor, and stormed out of the store. The rest of us, awkwardly, looked at each other and then, almost on cue, came out from our hiding places to pick up what was on the floor and comfort the young lady behind the counter.

Have you ever been in a situation like this, whether the customer or the clerk? Do not allow shame to intrude on your thoughts. Resist shame's whispers and continue reading. In fact, here's a prayer, inspired by 2 Corinthians 10:5, to help you resist the accuser of the brethren:

> *Father, in Jesus' name, I ask that you silence the accuser and destroy every spec-ulation and lofty thought that raises itself up against the truth and knowledge of God, and I take every thought captive to make it obedient to Christ. Amen.*

What the heck happened that made a grown woman, who appeared to be well-to-do, descend into a screaming fit? Was it the salesclerk? Was it the issue at hand? Was it something I did? No, no, and no. In counseling there is a phrase that says, "The issue is rarely the issue." Her meltdown probably had nothing to do with anything that happened that day. It most likely happened so long ago that she didn't even remember it.

Therapists have a great word to describe why people act the way they do: stuck. Observing the woman throwing her tantrum, a therapist might say that somewhere around the age of five that woman got stuck. In other words, the reason a grown woman is acting like a five-year-old may be a result of something traumatic that happened to her at the age she is now manifesting. If a young child experiences something traumatic, it stands to reason that they will process the incident (or accident) at whatever age they are at the time. Young children rarely have the capacity to think and reason like a mature adult. Without some guidance—and in some cases, counseling—the conclusion the child comes to will follow them into adolescence and even to adulthood. Therapists, counselors, psychologists, etc., go to great lengths to help adults recover from being stuck.

I use a slightly different word. Because I see pictures instead of words, I use the phrase "Somewhere, somehow, someone pushed your pause button." In order to fully appreciate this, you need to know about a particular type of cassette player. I had a great stereo system in my younger days that included a dual-cassette player and recorder. When the pause button was on, no other function—be it play, fast forward, rewind, or stop—would override it. Only when the pause button was pressed a second time would the player become unpaused. So no matter how many times I pressed or how hard I held down the play button, if the pause button was still engaged, the music would come out distorted, stunted, and warped.

When traumatic events happen in our lives, especially at a young age, it's as if our pause button has been pressed, and no matter how hard we try to "soldier on" and move forward, the way we see ourselves and the world around us can become distorted, stunted, and warped. This warping can also result in a state of being on-alert when a situation or circumstance reminds us of a traumatic event. This feeling of being on-alert is even more intense if someone has been abused or molested. To use a superhero metaphor, our Spidey-sense kicks in. No one else around us senses anything, but our skin is crawling, our breathing becomes labored, and others start asking us what's wrong when they see us reverting to the actions of a frightened child.

With the help of a psychologist, I was able to go back and deal with some of my most shameful and terrifying memories. Galatians says,

Brothers and sisters, if someone is caught in a sin, you who live by the Spirit should restore that person gently. But watch yourselves, or you also may be tempted. Carry each other's burdens, and in this way you will fulfill the law of Christ. If anyone thinks they are something when they are not, they deceive themselves.
—Galatians 6:1–3

What is interesting about this passage is that understanding the meaning of just one word changes the dynamic of these verses. The word "caught" is better translated as "overtaken or traumatized by something they were not prepared for." That is why an otherwise normal adult can revert back to acting like a child when something triggers the memories or feelings associated with something that overtook or traumatized them for which they were not prepared. And, as if right on cue, shame is there to distort the event and write a narrative on our hearts and souls that causes us to turn away from the light and cover up.

It's remarkable how many adults are released from the grip of shame when they go back and visit the moment when the pause button was pressed and realize how their pattern of thinking was established and reinforced over time.

32.

The Ruts of Shame

On the journey out of shame, we also need to be diligent about staying out. It is not unusual for people who have been set free from shame to revert back to patterns of thinking or into relationships that allow shame to enter their lives. Sadly, when this happens, it becomes harder to re-break the cycle of shame. Jesus taught us:

> *When an impure spirit comes out of a person, it goes through arid places seeking rest and does not find it. Then it says, "I will return to the house I left." When it arrives, it finds the house unoccupied, swept clean and put in order. Then it goes and takes with it seven other spirits more wicked than itself, and they go in and live there. And the final condition of that person is worse than the first.*
> —Matthew 12:43–45

Let me give an imperfect but otherwise helpful example. It's extremely difficult to encourage someone to quit smoking when you had already helped them quit smoking years earlier. All the statistics and logic that you used to make your case in the past, they already know. In fact, they will most likely mouth along with your lecture, because they've heard it all before and still made the decision to smoke. Another example is when you share with a Christian who no longer believes. They know the scriptures by heart and already know what you're going to say.

When someone gets free from shame, there is an initial euphoric feeling of weight being lifted off. But thought patterns are hard to break, and in order to make new and lasting change, we need to create new and healthy thought patterns.

Neurologists and psychiatrists refer to repeated thought patterns as schemas. These schemas are basically ruts, which our thoughts create in our brain. Once these ruts appear, caused by repeated thoughts, they begin to affect our patterns of behavior. If it's taken a lifetime of thinking to dig these ruts, there is no quick fix. We need to consistently and repeatedly retrain our brain.

Do not conform to the pattern of this world, but be transformed by the renewing of your mind.

—Romans 12:2

It doesn't take much for us to trip up and fall back into the rut of shameful thinking. Unless we begin building a fence, or clearly defined boundary, for our thoughts, the edge of the rut we escaped from will be sloped. There will be no cliff to define the edge from the bottom of the rut.

Memorizing and meditating on scripture is fundamental to creating new patterns of thinking. The simple and practical act of repetitively quoting scripture, until it is committed to memory, naturally creates new thought patterns. And what better words of affirmation are there than the ones spoken by our Creator? Here are just a few scriptures to begin building thought boundaries and new thought patterns.

"For I know the plans I have for you," declares the Lord, "plans to prosper you and not to harm you, plans to give you hope and a future. Then you will call on me and come and pray to me, and I will listen to you. You will seek me and find me when you seek me with all your heart."

—Jeremiah 29:11–13

For we are God's handiwork, created in Christ Jesus to do good works, which God prepared in advance for us to do.

—Ephesians 2:10

I praise you because I am fearfully and wonderfully made; your works are wonderful, I know that full well.

—Psalm 139:14

See what great love the Father has lavished on us, that we should be called children of God! And that is what we are!

—1 John 3:1

The Lord will make you the head, not the tail. If you pay attention to the commands of the Lord your God that I give you this day and carefully follow them, you will always be at the top, never at the bottom.

—Deuteronomy 28:13

I know what it is to be in need, and I know what it is to have plenty. I have learned the secret of being content in any and every situation, whether well fed or hungry, whether living in plenty or in want. 13 I can do all this through him who gives me strength.

—Philippians 4:12–13

Along with scripture, we may need to write a new life script from which to read from and quote. Speaking of life scripts, the next chapter is all about that.

33.

Life Scripts

"I'm ready for my close-up, Mr. DeMille."
—Gloria Swanson, as Norma Desmond, *Sunset Boulevard*[9]

AS A COMEDIAN AND ACTOR, THERE ARE TIMES IN MY PROFESSION WHEN I'VE HAD TO become another person or character. When I get a script, I not only read the lines that are highlighted for me, but I also read the whole script to find out what motivations are behind my character's words, responses, and actions.

Several years ago, I had to do a scene that required me to cry. After several takes, one of the production assistants came over and whispered in my ear, "How do you do that? Are you thinking of something in your life that makes you sad?"

My answer surprised them: "No."

When I get the opportunity to act, I try to become the character and react the way the character would feel and act, not the way I would feel and act. This ability to become a character is a result of more than acting classes. I'd spent a lifetime honing this skill.

Like most, if not all, people, I had a life script (things I believed about myself) that I read from as a child, adolescent, and then even as a grownup. Though some of the harsh and unloving words burnished on the pages of my life script were partly written by the hands of others, I believed them, ruminated on them, and ultimately even became them. I had assumed that I was just a co-writer of my life script and had to go along with whatever came my way, and occasionally add to what others had already written. What I came to realize was that I was the head writer! I effortlessly wrote harsh and unloving things that I believed about myself and memorized them.

---

9 *Sunset Boulevard*, directed by Billy Wilder (Los Angeles, CA: Paramount Pictures, 1950).

Like being able to recall word-for-word the lyrics to songs we haven't heard since high school, we are likewise capable of recalling memorized negative feelings and beliefs about ourselves. Though we may not have ever purposely or consciously thought of them, these negative inner dialogues can come flooding back because of a sound, smell, taste, word, or even someone's name. Once we hear the familiar tune of shame, feeling and beliefs come rushing back, and in a moment our mood turns dark and cloudy and we blithely sing along.

But wait. Have you ever been singing along with your car stereo and someone in the car says, "That's not what the words are."

"What?" you say. "I've been singing it this way forever! And now you tell me I've got it wrong? How could I do that?"

Well, it's because of what we heard and how we heard it. There are times when we mishear or misunderstand what someone said or did, so we rewrite their words, actions, or intent to fit our life script narrative. It could well be that we are missing out on something wonderful, because we didn't understand.

Similar to an actor preparing for a scene, we will memorize lines and then rehearse and rehearse and rehearse… and sadly, we rehearse lines and dialogue that may not be true.

When I became a Christian, the most difficult verses of the Bible for me to believe had nothing to do with the miracles Jesus performed, Jonah in the belly of a large fish, or three guys in a fiery furnace coming out unharmed. The difficult verses were the ones that said I was someone valuable, someone special, someone worth dying for, someone who had a destiny. These verses were diametrically opposed to my life script. Lines that I had memorized and rehearsed were being challenged. It would take all the faith I could muster to believe that Scripture trumped my script.

There are times when we need correction or even rebuke. When done incorrectly or with the absence of love and compassion, it comes across as disapproval and criticism. I've had my share of these.

Fortunately, I have also been the recipient of gentle, loving, and compassionate correction, and even a rebuke or two. But like mishearing the actual lyrics of a song, it took me a while to unlearn my script when someone offered correction. I often misheard it as disapproval or rejection and reinserted my own lyrics. I knew that my lyrics were somewhat off, but after years and years of attuning my ears to what I'd written, it took a while for the correct lyrics to replace the ones I had memorized. (You might notice that if you memorized the wrong words to a song, you often still sing them even when you know the right words.)

In addition to going back and dealing with my pause button, I've had to go back and request a rewrite of my life script. I don't want to become some character I was never meant to be, and I certainly don't want to give other people control over my script.

So I resigned as the head writer and tore up the application to even be a co-writer. I invited a much better writer to handle the rewrite. I hope you will, too.

...fixing our eyes on Jesus, the pioneer and perfecter of faith.

—Hebrews 12:2

34

Putting It into Practice

For the rest of our lives, we will always have opportunities to allow shame to move back in with us. We need to remain as diligent as someone recovering from addiction. Just one drink, one cigarette, one visit to a porn site can undo years of sobriety and living in victory over that which seeks to control us. As recovering addicts will tell you, they have to say no to the offers of "just one," because one can lead to many. In the same way, shame wants to undo years of sobriety and victory by inviting us to try on that iron coat for old time's sake.

Here's a recent example in my life. A few months ago, I was sitting backstage, listening to a preshow video and waiting to hear my cue to go onstage. Even after more than thirty years doing stand-up, it's not unusual to have preshow butterflies, but tonight was different. Tonight's butterflies felt more like the condors I used to experience in my early days in comedy clubs. And these condors were inviting me to entertain shame. I had less than twenty seconds to decide whether to go on stage for this Toronto show or run for the exit. Oh well, the show must go on—so on I went, but tonight's show was going to have some brand new material.

Before I can move forward with this, I need to go back in time. Not very far, mind you... in fact, I only need to go back a few hours, to the moment I shut the trunk of my car in the parking lot at the Atlanta's Hartsfield-Jackson International Airport. I felt a pang of shame and realized I had done something stupid, something I have never done before... ever. I had left my passport at home. I'm not sure why it hit me at that moment, because there were many other moments that it could have registered with me. It could have been when I was about to leave my house or maybe on the thirty-minute drive to the airport... heck, it could have even been while I was packing the night before, but nope, it was at the airport.

As I ran to catch the shuttle that would take me to the terminal, mentally kicking myself, I called my wife. Usually she takes me to the airport, but this was a fairly short trip, and I was on a very early flight. My wife is not what you would call a morning person, so calling her with the "good news" about my passport was not going to go over well. After the first few attempts to reach her went to voicemail, she finally answered sleepily, "Huh… hullo?"

"Honey, I need you to bring my passport to the new international terminal at the airport!" I stammered. "And hurry, because my flight leaves in less than an hour!"

I will spare you the details of the rest of our conversation. Suffice to say, Honey was not happy, and I was not in shape to run through the airport. Not only was I battling the thought of being an idiot for forgetting my passport, I was now berating myself about my weight… and it was about to get even worse.

As I approached the ticket counter with my luggage, my face must have said it all.

"You're not having a good morning are you?" asked the ticket agent.

I shared the story with her and asked if I could check in on an international flight without my passport.

I might as well have asked if I could fly the plane, too. She was polite, helpful, and even sympathetic, but rules are rules. She also informed me that the chances of my wife bringing my passport in time to board were slim to none. She recommended I take another flight to Toronto. Problem was, I would then arrive in Toronto after the show, so she suggested I fly to Buffalo, New York instead. And of course there would be a fee. Nope, check that; since my original ticket was to an international destination, I had to purchase a whole new ticket for a domestic destination. Not only was I an idiot for forgetting my passport, I added additional shame by wasting several hundred dollars. Oh boy, I couldn't wait to tell my wife.

Oh yeah, I thought. *I better call her, because I had to take the shuttle from the new international terminal to the old domestic terminal.*

After several failed attempts to reach her on her mobile phone, she finally answered and cried, "I'm lost!"

"Honey, I need you to meet me at the domestic terminal. I am flying to Buffalo, New York."

A thoughtful husband would have paused to take in what his wife had said and how she'd said it, but running again through the airport, dragging luggage, tends to make one less than thoughtful. I will, again, spare you the details of our conversation. Suffice to say, Honey wanted to resign from my fan club, and I was at full panic, because to top it all off her mobile phone was dying—and she didn't have a charger in the car.

Shame was not only working me over, that jerk was working over my wife. In attempting to bring my passport to the new international terminal, she'd gotten lost, because she had never driven there before. The more she couldn't find her way, the more shame whispered unkind and cruel lies—the same lies it whispered to me: "You're so stupid, what's wrong with you? Why can't you do anything right?"

By the time she arrived at the lower level, there was no way in the hot place I was going to get a goodbye kiss. In fact, the mere gesture of not running me over as she tossed my passport out the car window is a testimony to her love and grace. I would have totally understood if she had made me a hood ornament. And to top it all off, her phone was now completely dead. Well, time to get on the flight for another show—called "Couples Night Out," ironically—to celebrate marriage with love and laughter! Yay me!

For the next few hours, I had no way of communicating with Kathy. On the flight, my stomach was in knots. I ruminated about canceling the show and getting on the first flight back to Atlanta as soon as I landed in Buffalo. But I needed to pay for the new plane ticket. As the hours ticked by without being able to talk to her, I let my guard down and started entertaining shame's accusations. After my manager secured ground transportation from Buffalo to Toronto to meet up with the tour manager, I calculated that if I didn't eat anything, or visit Starbucks or Tim Horton's over the next few days, I would just about break even.

Finally, about an hour before the show, I was able to reach my wife via text. I tested the waters with a little humor and wrote, "You haven't contacted an attorney, have you?" to which she replied in kind: "We can't afford one." I will spare you the rest of our textersation. Suffice to say, Honey was gracious, and I was grateful.

So here I was about to walk out to an expectant audience, who were ready to laugh and be encouraged about how to have a lasting and loving marriage, and even then, shame was still nipping at me like a crazed Chihuahua. Finally, I said rather loudly, "Enough!"

Fortunately there was no one else backstage, because I also pointed as if I were poking someone in the chest. Once more I spoke out loud: "In Jesus' name, enough!" I snapped out of my funk just as the preshow video gave way to the voiceover intro.

"Ladies and gentlemen… please welcome from Atlanta, Georgia…"

I was finally able to go onstage and leave my once familiar iron coat behind.

Usually it takes a while for people to "look back at this and laugh," but I only had a few more seconds to find the humor. So that night, I added a new comedy bit that was honest, authentic, and a little more than poignant. I am so glad I did, because that night after the show I had conversations with several couples that had fought on their way to the show. I will spare you the details of those conversations. Suffice to say, Kathy was glad when I came home, and I was happy we couldn't afford an attorney.

Shame doesn't stand a chance when you shine a light on it, speak truth over it, and walk on from it... in Jesus' name.

35.

Free to Forgive

WITH THE EXCEPTION OF THE CHAPTER "THE WHITEBOARD," YOU MAY HAVE WONDERED why I waited until now to address forgiveness specifically. We both know darn good and well that if I had started out writing about forgiveness, there was a fifty-fifty chance you would have stopped reading. And for that matter, that I would have stopped writing! Why? Well, because I am still in the process of forgiving some people. I am not an expert on forgiveness nor have I arrived as the great forgiver.

Forgiveness is hard! It's like tithing. Practicing the discipline of tithing, when you have a lot of money, is just as hard as when you have little money. When you have a lot of money, your tithe check could also purchase a brand new car. When you have little money, your tithe check is a tank of gas for your car.

Then there's the discipline of forgiveness. Discipline? Why discipline? Because forgiving is like eating right, exercising, avoiding gossip, brushing your teeth, getting to bed on time, and not hitting the snooze button ten times... it's a choice. We choose to eat right, exercise, avoid gossip, brush our teeth, and so on. Likewise, we choose to forgive. God does not make us forgive; He doesn't make us believe in His existence, accept His Son as our Savior, or even tithe. So why would He then start making us do things like forgiving people? He doesn't! *He invites us to.* Like the invitation to accept His grace by faith, we are invited to forgive by faith and not by feelings.

Shame says, "Heck no! Don't forgive them! They don't deserve to be forgiven!" Sounds good to me. I guess shame is making some sense now and is even on my side. Uh-huh, yeah. And just so you'll know, shame is taking their side, too. The very words and tactics that shame uses to convince you not to forgive are used against you when others have reason to forgive you. What a traitor!

A result of shame, whether we have been shamed or have shamed others, is that the effects are the same. We don't feel that those who shamed us deserve to be forgiven. If we are very, very honest with ourselves, deep down, we don't feel that we deserve to be forgiven, either. Shame attacks our ability to believe that God completely and unconditionally loves us.

So how do we do this? Why now, near the end of this book, does forgiveness get addressed? Well, there are two people who were near the end of their lives and showed an amazing display of forgiveness that changed my perception and understanding of forgiveness. Jesus and Stephen. Actually, it all started in the Garden of Gethsemane, when Jesus spoke to Judas, who had betrayed Him for thirty pieces of silver:

Jesus replied, "Do what you came for, friend."
—Matthew 26:50

Friend? Jesus called that so-and-so His friend? Now we know that Jesus truly was supernatural! Though Judas was not faithful to Jesus, Jesus was faithful to Judas. And then on the cross, Jesus says, regarding those who abandoned, falsely accused, tortured, mocked, shamed, spit on, berated, pounded a crown of thorns into his brow, stripped him naked, and then drove nails into his hands and feet:

"Father, forgive them, for they do not know what they are [really] doing."
—Luke 23:34

Jesus was supernatural, indeed. He had to use every ounce of His deity to pull that off. And He did so, as a man:

Who, being in very nature God, did not consider equality with God something to be used to his own advantage; rather, he made himself nothing by taking the very nature of a servant, being made in human likeness. And being found in appearance as a man, he humbled himself by becoming obedient to death—even death on a cross!
—Philippians 2:6–8

Jesus laid His deity aside and did all that as a man. What a good role model for a young man named Stephen.

Acts 6 describes a very tense situation that arose in the early church concerning the daily distribution of food among the Grecian and Hebraic widows. The Grecians felt slighted, so the Hebraic leaders got together and chose seven men from among the Grecian and Hebraic believers to oversee the daily distribution of food. They chose all Grecian Christians. Among them was a young man named Stephen.

Like his Lord and Savior, Stephen was falsely accused, mocked, shamed, and mistreated by religious zealots and yet had the same attitude as Jesus:

While they were stoning him, Stephen prayed, "Lord Jesus, receive my spirit." Then he fell on his knees and cried out, "Lord, do not hold this sin against them." When he had said this, he fell asleep.

—Acts 7:59–60

Stephen was able to forgive them in the moment—not after some time had passed, not after he talked about it with his support group, but in the moment. How? Can I make one small observation that may be what gave Stephen the supernatural ability to forgive? Take a look at verses 55–56:

But Stephen, full of the Holy Spirit, looked up to heaven and saw the glory of God, and Jesus standing at the right hand of God. "Look," he said, "I see heaven open and the Son of Man standing at the right hand of God."

—Acts 7:55–56

Notice that he says, *"I see heaven open and the Son of man standing at the right hand of God."* This is the only time in scripture that we see Jesus "standing" at the right hand of God. Every other reference in the Bible where Jesus is at the right hand of His Father, He is "sitting." (Now that right there is a sermon for some of the pastors and teachers who are reading this.) Can you imagine the supernatural impact that seeing Jesus stand up had on Stephen? Can you imagine the supernatural impact seeing that would have on you?

When I read this account and then read the conversation that Peter and Jesus had in Matthew 18, I begin to see that forgiveness is as much supernatural as it is a choice or act of our free will. Only when we get the revelation that Jesus—who became sin for us by taking our sin, guilt, shame, and punishment upon Himself—died upon the cross can we truly understand what true forgiveness really is.

Then Peter came to Jesus and asked, "Lord, how many times shall I forgive my brother or sister who sins against me? Up to seven times?"

Jesus answered, "I tell you, not seven times, but seventy-seven times.

"Therefore, the kingdom of heaven is like a king who wanted to settle accounts with his servants. As he began the settlement, a man who owed him ten thousand bags of gold was brought to him. Since he was not able to pay, the master ordered that he and his wife and his children and all that he had be sold to repay the debt.

"At this the servant fell on his knees before him. 'Be patient with me,' he begged, 'and I will pay back everything.' The servant's master took pity on him, canceled the debt and let him go.

"But when that servant went out, he found one of his fellow servants who owed him a hundred silver coins. He grabbed him and began to choke him. 'Pay back what you owe me!' he demanded.

"His fellow servant fell to his knees and begged him, 'Be patient with me, and I will pay it back.'

"But he refused. Instead, he went off and had the man thrown into prison until he could pay the debt. When the other servants saw what had happened, they were outraged and went and told their master everything that had happened.

"Then the master called the servant in. 'You wicked servant,' he said, 'I canceled all that debt of yours because you begged me to. Shouldn't you have had mercy on your fellow servant just as I had on you?' In anger his master handed him over to the jailers to be tortured, until he should pay back all he owed.

"This is how my heavenly Father will treat each of you unless you forgive your brother or sister from your heart."

—Matthew 18:21–35

The wicked servant that Jesus told Peter about was wicked not because of murder, theft, or lying, but because he would not forgive a small debt that was owed to him even though he had been forgiven a large debt that he himself could never repay.

With this revelation of what forgiveness is, we can truly understand how powerful forgiveness toward others is, and even the forgiveness that we need to extend to ourselves.

So if the Son sets you free, you will be free indeed.

—John 8:36

36.

Lessons from a Flawed King

KING DAVID IS ONE OF THE MOST BELOVED, WHILE AT THE SAME TIME CONTROVERSIAL, personalities in all of Scripture. His courage, good deeds, and love for God are well-documented, as well as his dark side, which led him to commit adultery with Bathsheba and then cover up the affair by, in effect, signing her husband's death warrant. And yet he's known as a man after God's own heart and wrote the majority of the book of Psalms.

Rather than deal with all of David's misdeeds and failures, I want to focus on what it was that allowed him to avoid being crippled by shame... the shame that came from others as well as the shame of his own actions, flaws, and failures.

It begins with understanding that God doesn't see people as we see people. Remember that when Samuel was dispatched to Jesse's house to anoint a new king, it was a result of Saul's desire to please man instead of pleasing God (1 Samuel 13–15), which cost him not only the throne, but God's favor as well. Upon arriving at Jesse's house and seeing his sons, Samuel was impressed, but Samuel was about to learn a lesson about judging a book by its cover.

> *When they arrived, Samuel saw Eliab and thought, "Surely the Lord's anointed stands here before the Lord."*
>
> *But the Lord said to Samuel, "Do not consider his appearance or his height, for I have rejected him. The Lord does not look at the things people look at. People look at the outward appearance, but the Lord looks at the heart."*
>
> —1 Samuel 16:6–7

God expounds on this a bit when He addresses another great prophet, telling him,

Shameless

"For my thoughts are not your thoughts, neither are your ways my ways," declares the Lord. "As the heavens are higher than the earth, so are my ways higher than your ways and my thoughts than your thoughts.

—Isaiah 55:8–9

Just like Samuel and Isaiah, we, too, are tempted to think that God thinks like we do and sees people and circumstance the way we do. It's an age-old variation on a popular theme: "Let us create God in our image."

Jesse had no idea what was coming that day he went to Jesse's house. He was probably under the impression that he was going to choose who was worthy of being anointed king. It also seems to me that because of the way Jesse saw his sons, he may have been reluctant to present one of them in particular to Samuel. You know, the one who wrote poetry, played a lyre, and sang to sheep.

Jesse had seven of his sons pass before Samuel, but Samuel said to him, "The Lord has not chosen these." So he asked Jesse, "Are these all the sons you have?"

"There is still the youngest," Jesse answered. "He is tending the sheep."

Samuel said, "Send for him; we will not sit down until he arrives."

So he sent for him and had him brought in. He was glowing with health and had a fine appearance and handsome features.

Then the Lord said, "Rise and anoint him; this is the one."

—1 Samuel 16:10–12

David's own father didn't seem to consider him a candidate to appear before Samuel. How crushing is that? After God rejects every son that Samuel saw as worthy, he asks Jesse, almost as if in frustration, *"Are these all the sons you have?"* To which Jesse replies, *"There is still the youngest, but he is tending the sheep"* (1 Samuel 16:11).

I almost hear Jesse's response this way: "Yeah, I have one more son, but he's just a shepherd, and he's a musician. He has long hair and some tattoos, and he writes poetry." I wonder if anyone has ever made you feel less than. I know that I have.

David faithfully served his father, and he also tried to faithfully serve his brothers, but their view of him was not heaven's view, either. Remember the story about hat giant dude?

Samuel writes that when Jesse sent his son David to check on his brothers, who were currently at a stalemate with the Philistines and fearing that guy named Goliath, his brothers took offense at him. David was simply following his father's order to bring back word about his other sons, as well as bring along some roasted grain, bread, and cheese… for them! Here's an older brother's take on David showing up:

When Eliab, David's oldest brother, heard him speaking with the men, he burned with anger at him and asked, "Why have you come down here? And with whom did you leave those few sheep in the wilderness? I know how conceited you are and how wicked your heart is; you came down only to watch the battle."

—1 Samuel 17:28

What's amazing is how David handles this accusation:

"Now what have I done?" said David. "Can't I even speak?" He then turned away to someone else and brought up the same matter, and the men answered him as before.

—1 Samuel 17:29–30

Even though his brothers, notably Eliab, had their own opinions of him, David knew,

Like a fluttering sparrow or a darting swallow, an undeserved curse does not come to rest.

—Proverbs 26:2

David resisted the shame that could have come as a result of his own father's reluctance to send for him when Samuel came calling. He resisted the negative opinions and beliefs that his brothers had of him. We likewise need to resist the shame that can come when others don't see the best in us (or even anything good).

What mattered most to David was how God saw him. Even in the best of families, we typically default to our human and earthly viewpoint. It's so easy to think poorly of ourselves, and then when others see us poorly, it's all the confirmation we need to fall further down the bottomless pit of despair.

It can happen when a coach doesn't think we're good enough to make the team, or when a teacher, youth pastor, or another person we look to for affirmation thinks we're a lost cause. Then we lose sight of God's view and begin seeking to please people rather than the God who created us. Shame has a cruel way of making us believe the untrue and negative things that those we seek approval from believe about us.

37.

Alice at Last

Gentlemen, the only way to achieve the impossible is to think that it is possible.
—Charles Kingsley, *Alice in Wonderland*[10]

I LOVE A GOOD STORY, ESPECIALLY STORIES WHERE THE LEAST LIKELY CHARACTER IS THE hero and there is an underlying spiritual truth. And I really love it when Hollywood bumps into the truth.

Cinema has always been a medium that speaks to me. Reading is not my strength, and there are too many distractions while watching television. Watching films in a theater, however, transports me, which has caused my children to be reluctant to attend movies with me. I tend to be affected more than the usual patrons.

I've been known to embarrass my family by crying in movie theaters when a film touches on a biblical truth. A few years ago, I took my daughter to see a movie, and about halfway through she looked over at me, saw my tears, and whispered, "Really, Dad? Again?"

All I could do was nod and continue watching *Alice in Wonderland*.

In Tim Burton's 2010 film version, he revisits Lewis Carroll's two classic stories, *Alice's Adventures in Wonderland* and its sequel *Through the Looking-Glass and What Alice Found There*. In the film, Alice Kinsley, now an adult, has returned to Wonderland, but has no memory of being there as a child and believes she is dreaming. Having been on a quest to find the "right Alice," the White Rabbit has returned Alice to Wonderland by prompting her to chase after him and then tumbling down the rabbit hole.

An assortment of Wonderland creatures begin gathering around Alice to see if she is the "right Alice" and then conclude that she is the "wrong Alice." The White Rabbit maintains that she is in fact the "right Alice." The debate continues

---

10 *Alice in Wonderland*, directed by Tim Burton (Los Angeles, CA: Walt Disney Pictures, 2010).

until it is decided that Alice will appear before Absalom, the blue caterpillar, as he will know whether or not she is the "right Alice."

In the film, Alice appears before the blue caterpillar three separate times, and each of these visits come at a pivotal moment. And each time the caterpillar has something to say that's more about how Alice views herself than how others see her.

At their first meeting, when everyone is asking if she is the "right Alice," Absalom's response is "Not hardly." During her second meeting with him, she is told that she is much more Alice than she used to be. As the film draws toward its climactic conclusion, Absalom proclaims to her that she is "Alice at last."

Sitting there in the theater, fighting back tears so as not to embarrass my daughter at a movie, again, I thought of my own journey and how it seemed similar to Alice's. Like the main character, I knew financial distress, I have family dynamics that are hard to face, and I've had other people tell me what I should do with my life—and according to them, what they felt was best for me. It was this line—"You're much more Alice than you used to be"—that got me.

When I think back on my life, treading carefully to avoid shame attacks, I look to moments when I was first doing stand-up and would introduce myself to someone. When I said, "Hi, I'm Steve Geyer," I wonder if heaven whispered, "Not hardly." I am free and unashamed to tell you that when I first started out in comedy, I was a mess—insecure, selfish, and envious... and those were my good traits. I suffered almost crippling stage fright and would not be able to eat for eight hours prior to going onstage. Yet every night I'd muster the strength to risk being rejected by yet another audience.

After becoming a Christian, I continued in comedy, but was still a mess. Insecure, self-focused, and petty were my new good traits. I loved Jesus, but I loved approval just as much—if not more. I was fortunate, in those years, to be mentored by several men who poured into me the traits that would manifest in me years later. To this day, I am eternally grateful for these men, who still have no idea how much they affected my life. When I look back on those years and recall introducing myself to others, I wonder if heaven instead whispers, "He's much more Steve than he used to be."

During their first meeting, Absalom called Alice a stupid girl, and she remained silent, but at their last meeting when he says it again she is no longer silent and replies, "I'm not stupid!" Okay, now I'm in the theater boo-hooing into my shirt, which I've pulled up over my nose and mouth. My daughter has found another row to sit in.

When Alice exclaimed that she wasn't stupid, I saw a little boy who looked a lot like me playing Frisbee in a front yard, just like the one I grew up in, and exclaiming, "I'm not Dumb Steve!" I thought of Mrs. Van Hooydonk, my tenth grade math teacher, telling me that I was smart. I thought of a moment on a mission trip, when someone pulled me aside and said, "Steve, you are brilliant in the way you prepared us for this trip," and a moment when someone I greatly admire said, "Steve, for a guy who dropped out of college, you are one of the most well-read people I know." For several minutes, I watched the movie as words of healthy affirmation cascaded over my heart, soul, and mind. It was glorious.

One more thing that Absalom says to Alice made me think of the Scriptures—when he tells Alice that all she has to do is hold onto the Vorpal Sword (with which she must defeat a dangerous beast known as the Jabberwocky) because "it knows what it wants to do."

Now that's a great line. Believing that the Bible is the Sword of the Spirit, all I have to do is hold onto the truths and teaching in God's Word—and He will accomplish in me what He set out to do, shame be danged!

In the grip and cyclical pattern of shame, if we were to introduce ourselves to the Creator of all things, He would probably respond, "Not hardly." As we identify areas of shame in our lives and begin our journey from darkness to light, His response would likely be, "You are much more you than you used to be." And over time, we may hear heaven whisper, "You, at last!"

Alice takes hold of her destiny as she grips the sword and faces the Jabberwocky. Once the Jabberwocky is slain, and all is right again in Wonderland, Alice is whisked back to the moment when she first fell down the rabbit hole.

Disheveled, scratched-up, and dirty, Alice tries to unrumple her dress. Everyone around her is gob-smacked at her appearance, but she confidently begins speaking and taking her choices out of the hands of others. She sees herself as responsible for her own choice. Whether right or wrong, they will be her decisions from now on.

Alice had a blue caterpillar to counsel her, but we have a much better Counselor: the Holy Spirit. We are heirs with Christ, and therefore we freely receive guidance from the God of the universe, whose grace is sufficient in our weakness. Like Absalom provoking Alice to fulfill her destiny, our Father compels us by His Spirit and the sacrifice of His only Son to *take hold of that for which Christ Jesus took hold [us]* (Philippians 3:12).

At times I believe we have all been "not hardly," which is a natural part of life. Sadly, some never move beyond being "not hardly." If we are to become "me, at last," it is up to us to take hold of our own destinies by yielding to God's Word and who He says we are. Paul states matter-of-factly, *"For we are God's hand-iwork, created in Christ Jesus to do good works, which God prepared in advance for us to do"* (Ephesians 2:10).

Certainly we are helped and hindered along our journey by others, but they are never the ones fully in control. Today is a good day to start becoming "much more you than you used to be" to "almost you" to "you, at last."

The Sword knows what it wants. All you have to do is hold on to it.

And Near the End...

I'VE ALWAYS LOVED A HAPPY ENDING, AND WITH THAT IN MIND I PURPOSELY DELAYED writing this final chapter. As I wrote in the disclaimer, this book has been very difficult to write. In fact, it was very hard to even start. Once I began writing, other difficulties presented themselves. There were rewrites, edits, more rewrites and edits, and because I had to revisit my past, there were days when I just wanted to press "Command-Option-Esc" (for PC users, "Ctrl-Alt-Delete") and be done with it. What kept me going were my family and the people involved in this process who encouraged and prayed for me, plus an editor who read this over and over again to ensure that what was in my heart and mind could be readable.

Mrs. Van Hooydonk was the first person who ever told me that I was smart, and I believed it. There have since been other people who came into my life to speak truth to me.

Jim Davis from Belmont Church gave me such a gentle rebuke that I didn't realize until much later it was a rebuke.

Don Harris, my dear friend in Plano, Texas, hurt but never harmed me with his velvet-covered-hammer rebuke. That encouraged me to *not* fight godly brokenness, but to desire and chase after it... and to never disguise my limp after my wrestling match with the Lord.

By this point, you've probably discerned that shame, in so many ways, produced in me the feeling and belief that I was fatherless. As a kid, I remember sitting on our front porch, imagining and even praying for my dad to drive up and rescue me. Alas, he never did and for a long time this affected my relationship with God the Father.

I embraced Jesus as the most amazing teacher, leader, fisherman, wine-maker, human-jungle-gym, and my Savior. I believed the Holy Spirit would infill and indwell me with wisdom and revelation, and I could hear His voice. But the

Father… hmm, I wasn't so sure about Him. I grew up believing that God was angry, and this belief hounded me for many years after my conversion to Christ.

More often than not, we project onto our Heavenly Father our feelings or beliefs regarding our relationship with our earthly fathers. And I am no exception.

For a very, very long time I held onto this fatherless mindset. Then three events happened in my life: the birth of my daughter, a conversation with my five-year-old son, and an encounter with a jolly tall man in a bright red jacket.

It Began with a Baby

Let me begin this concluding trilogy of stories by saying that I believe God still does speak to us—and will, if we have ears to hear. I believe we can hear with the ears of our heart and spirit and, on occasion, with our physical ears, too. Let me tell you a story about that.

When my wife and I were expecting our first child, I was filled with joy and dread at the same time. I was so excited to have a child, but terrified about being a father. I was afraid I would be a bad one. Oh, like most expectant couples, we read all the books, memorized all the dos and don'ts, went to birthing classes, and even preemptively childproofed our apartment in case our baby was born with the ability to walk. But none of the baby books talked about the heart of a father.

I wrestled with the notion that not only did my father divorce my mother, but that he never sought to see me or my siblings after the divorce. Remember, when I was a kid, shame compelled me to believe it was my fault that he left. Even as a grown man, I felt that somehow I was unfit to be loved—that Jesus was my friend, the Holy Spirit was my guide, but that my Heavenly Father would never approve of me.

I carried this belief deeply buried in my soul, and never spoke of these feelings to anyone… ever.

On Tuesday night, September 18, 1990, at 10:51 p.m. CST, the most beautiful baby girl entered this world and instantly changed me forever… and I do mean instantly. Initially, I only caught a glimpse of her, because she had a respiratory issue which required three technicians to attend to her and block my view. I remember every detail, even down to what I was wearing and what the lead nurse's name was. What I remember most is how I felt.

For those who have experienced the miracle of childbirth, I hope you can relate to what I am about to write.

As I stood frozen in the middle of the labor and delivery room, I could feel my heartbeat in my ears. The technicians worked feverishly to clear my baby's airway so that she could breathe. I wasn't sure what she looked like; I had no clue if she had any hair.

I was almost certain that she would have blue eyes (at least for the first three months) and really hoped that she would look like her mommy. And yet there I stood—frozen, overwhelmed, and completely in love with someone whom I still hadn't officially met.

Then I prayed, "Oh, God, please help my baby, and let her live… please!" At that moment I knew that no matter her personality, gifts, talents, or eventual eye color, I would give my life for this child. I had never experienced a feeling like this before. It was if, hidden in my heart, there was a chamber that God unlocked, and my daughter was the key.

Finally, after what seemed like forever, one of the technicians placed in my arms a tiny, swaddled, perfectly breathing baby and said, "Congratulations, Mr. Geyer, here is your baby girl."

Much of the shame I battled had to do with the feeling and belief that even though God loves me, I still need to get busy earning His love and proving that I love Him back. I never truly rested in His love and amazing grace. Once I believed, I got busy! I had so much to learn, so much to repent of, so much to make right, and so very much to do to get caught up on all those wasted years. It was enough to drive a guy crazy… and it almost did.

I knew from the Scriptures that I had a destiny, so I sought diligently to *"take hold of that for which Christ Jesus took hold of me"* (Philippians 3:12). But I never really stopped to ponder my purpose. If I had, I might have shaken off shame a lot sooner. You see, the purpose of me being created was so that God could love me. Period. The end. Th–th–th–that's all, folks!

Stop! Don't you even say it… not yet anyway.

Most likely, after you read my purpose statement, you immediately felt led to add an "and" or a "but," followed by a verse about pleasing God. I, too, want to please God! But can you tarry a moment, pondering in your heart that God's purpose for creating you was so that He could love you? Shame says, "No!" In fact, it says, "Hell no!" Shame won't let you enjoy the fact that our birth actually fulfilled our purpose, which then makes our destiny something to strive for rather than to rest in.

Shame produces fear in us that we need to do something to earn God's love, but remember that His perfect love drives out that fear! Shame causes us to have an external love relationship with God, as if it's something we need to find hanging in our closet. Colossians 1:27 states, *"Christ in [me is] the hope of glory."*

So, if I have this straight, I don't live *for* Jesus, I actually live *from* Jesus. And I don't have to work *for* Jesus, I work *from* Jesus. God is not a jacket or cruel taskmaster; He *is* love and is supernaturally loving me from the inside-out. Wow!

Now, you should know that I really want to please God, and reading the scriptures I know that *"without faith it is impossible to please God…"* (Hebrews 11:6)

So here's a thought: what if my first real act of faith is truly believing that *"by grace [I] have been saved, though faith… not by works"* (Ephesians 2:8–9) and *"[w]hile [I was] still [a sinner], Christ died for [me]"* (Romans 5:8)? And how about even really believing that *"God so loved the world that he gave his one and only Son, that whoever believes in him shall not perish but have eternal life"* (John 3:16)?

If I truly believe those scriptures, I can be satisfied that I have already achieved my purpose and am now free to fulfill my destiny, which He's already planned out (Jeremiah 29:11).

As I stood, still frozen, holding Kirsten Noel Geyer, I had a hard time seeing her features. Tears of joy, mixed with revelation, filled my eyes and dropped onto her striped newborn blanket, which all hospitals use. The tears were not simply a result of relief that she was okay. They were not because I was tired, even though I was. They were the response of God's voice, which penetrated my heart so deeply that I heard them in my ears.

As I held Kirsten for the very first time, after enduring those moments of uncertainty concerning her breathing, and realizing that I was willing to give my life for her, I heard clearly and distinctly, "Stephen… this is exactly how I love you."

Selah. Stop. Pause. And think about that.

GI Joe®

The next story in this trilogy (I always wanted to write a trilogy) is about another God-made key that unlocked another hidden chamber in my heart.

I wonder how many guys remember playing with GI Joe, or how many will admit to it? Remember, GI Joe wasn't a doll… he was an army man! I openly and unapologetically confess many hours of fighting fictitious enemy soldiers and weaponry, poised to eliminate the good ole U.S. of A., and having my GI Joe save the day. I loved my GI Joe. And I'm not talking about that wimpy little four-inch action figure that came out in the 70s and 80s; I'm talking about the original.

Twelve inches, scar-faced, real, metal, dog tags, and fully pose-able… it was the best boy toy ever!

Growing up in my neighborhood, you were called by name, but known for what GI Joe or related accessories you had. It was not uncommon to refer to a guy by name or by GI Joe gear. "Hey, you guys know Billy with the Green Beret GI Joe…?"

I hadn't thought of GI Joe for years, until on my way home from a comedy tour, I was looking for gifts to bring home to my children. Shopping back then was easy for my daughter… she liked Beanie Babies®! My son was a bit more difficult to buy for.

On the drive to the airport in Austin, Texas, I asked the driver if he could take me to a shopping center or mall. He took me to Target. He dropped me off at the door, and as I was about to sprint to the toy department, I spotted something right at the front of the store that I hadn't seen since I was a kid. It was a full-sized GI Joe. I couldn't believe it! Hasbro had rereleased a full-sized GI Joe with all four branches of the military from which to choose. There was the Army, Air Force, Navy, and Marines. I couldn't decide which one to get. So I bought all four.

Upon returning home, my wife informed me that our son was too young (and I was too old) to play with them. After much protesting, I decided to store them in Santa's workshop: our attic. I confess that from time to time, when I was in the attic for one reason or another, I would take one of the GI Joes out of his box and… what's the word… oh, yeah, I'd play with it. I do hope my wife never reads this.

Finally, after a year and a half of GI Joes in lockdown, my son was going to get his first real GI Joe for Christmas. I could hardly sleep that Christmas Eve. Christmas morning finally arrived, and we opened his presents together. We carefully removed all the little accessories, making sure that none were lost. It was the classic Army man in green battle gear, complete with helmet, rifle, hand grenades, and canteen. He next opened the Air Force pilot. "Wow, Dad, he's got goggles and everything!" He was thrilled, and to tell you the truth, so was I. Later that night, Graham slept securely in his bed with his GI Joes standing watch in the night.

A few months after Christmas, my son and I were in his room playing a game. Since we were not playing with his GI Joes at the time, his question puzzled me: "Daddy, you like GI Joe a lot, don't you?"

Where in the world did that come from? I thought. I decided to answer his question with a question of my own. "Yes, I do, Graham. Why do you ask?"

"Oh, no reason."

"Does it bother you that I like him?"

"Oh no, Daddy, I like it… but why do *you* like him so much?"

As we knelt together over the game we were playing, that simple question, asked again, brought out intense emotions. It surprised me more than Graham that I began to cry.

"What's wrong, Daddy?" Graham asked as tears filled his eyes.

My son and daughter have always been sensitive to the feelings of others, even when those others are the ones who sometimes spanked their little bottoms. It took me a few seconds to regain my composure enough to give him the answer to his question—a question that reached into the dimmed recesses of my memory. It was a memory that up until now I had chosen to forget. I knew the answer, but I wasn't sure Graham would understand it.

"Son, when Daddy was a little boy, I didn't have a dad… and sometimes at night, I would get scared." Then I asked, "Graham, where do you go when you get scared at night?"

He looked up at me. "In bed with you."

"That's right, son, I'll always be there for you. But since I didn't have a dad, I would put my GI Joe in bed with me to protect me and keep me safe. He was like a best friend, and sometimes I would pretend that he was my dad."

Graham was now staring at the floor, and I thought to myself, *Great, just great… now the kid's going to need counseling!*

Without looking up at me, he asked, "You never got to kiss your dad?"

"No, I never did."

"You never got hugged by your dad?"

"No, son."

Graham sat silently for a moment and then leapt from his knees and grabbed me around the neck, so hard it almost knocked me over.

"That's not fair, Daddy," he cried. "That's not fair! I will always be there to hug and kiss you." Then he added, almost in a whisper, "And if you get scared, you can get in bed with me!"

Tears once again filled my eyes, but a smile came to my face at his invitation for sanctuary from the boogeyman.

Though I never experienced fatherhood from a son's point of view, with joy I now experience it from a father's. It was at this moment that I finally had an understanding of a verse that had been spoken over and over to me from the

Old Testament: *"I will repay you [says the Lord] for the years the locusts have eaten..."* (Joel 2:25)

I had forgiven my father many years ago for leaving us. But as Graham and I embraced in his room, I felt a peace come over me—a peace that let me release my father in a deeper way for not being there for me in the night.

I marveled that a simple Christmas present given to my son would usher in a peace that I could hardly explain. I marvel, even more, at the first Christmas present given: Immanuel, God with us. This is the true essence of Christmas, after all. God's greatest present is His presence.

As a kid, Graham took very good care of his GI Joes, even though there are a few with missing limbs. He even has some that he kept on shelves. Now that my son has a son, I'm ready for Christmases yet to come. You see, there were still two guys in the attic waiting for active duty.

Son Arise

The last story is about an unexpected blessing, which I never thought I deserved or could even earn.

While sitting in our church's café, chatting with a lovely woman who was visiting our church for the first time, a voice boomed from behind me: "What are you doing hitting on my wife!?" As the pastor of outreach and missions, it was my role to make certain that guests and first-time visitors were treated warmly. Heck, I was just doing my job.

With the fear of God coursing through my veins, I slowly turned around to address the booming voice. Behind me stood a huge—make that booming—man to match the booming voice. He was wearing a bright red sports jacket that would have made Santa Claus green with envy. Being a comic and a pastor all these years has equipped me with the knack of quickly assessing an audience, a situation, and crazy people.

I quickly determined that the Goliath in the bright red coat was in his seventies (his wife looked much, much, much... much younger), and though he could crush me like a grape, I figured that I could outrun him. I then noticed a wry smile on his wife's face and an unmistakable twinkle of mischief in his eyes, so I risked it all and replied, "Well, what do you expect? Leaving a beautiful woman like this all alone in a church? Some guy is going to offer to buy her a cup of coffee!"

There was a brief, silent pause that seemed to last a lot longer than it actually did. Before I could rethink my reply, both the redcoat and the lovely lady burst into laughter. After a sigh of relief and momentary check of my underpants, I joined in.

That was the day that I met Ken and Carolyn. I don't often recall the first time I meet someone. Those "remember the first time we met" moments are reserved for a few people in my life: my wife Kathy, my future in-laws, our children, my manager, dear friends, and Ken and Carolyn—or as they are known by their children and grandchildren, Paw-Paw and La-La.

What started with a boom turned into a friendship—one that found me, after fifteen-plus years off the court, playing tennis with a guy who I mistakenly assumed I could outrun. This friendship led to weekly conversations at Starbucks about American, world, and church history. Through this friendship I learned how to choose a fine wine and appreciate fine dining, all of which was a result of my fine friend.

Not only did I enjoy Ken's company, he seemingly enjoyed mine. I would expectantly wait for him to call or text me about coffee or tennis, because I didn't want to be a pest or get under his feet. When he would call or text, I'd be like a little kid waiting for his dad to come home from work. Hold the phone… I'm a grown man here and have kids of my own, yet I couldn't deny the joy I felt each time Ken contacted me.

Over the last few years, Ken and Carolyn became more than just a part of our lives; they became family. Kathy and I love spending time with them. Whether just sitting on their back deck or going out for fine dining, we enjoy just being with them. We don't really care where we go or if we go, just as long as we are with them. Ken and Carolyn have this effect on everyone they meet. They have a gift for making us feel like we are their very best friends, all while knowing that they treat *all* their friends this way.

A few years ago, I had a strange voicemail from Ken. It wasn't his usual playful tone; he was serious and said he needed to meet with me about something. Immediately my heart sank, and my old shame tapes began to play.

What did I do? I thought to myself as I dialed his number.

He answered with a playful, "Oh, were you screening your calls?"

I was relieved. He didn't seem angry and we chatted about nothing of consequence for a bit. Then he asked if I could meet him at Starbucks that day at 2:30 p.m. because he wanted to ask me a couple of questions and that he was going to "stump" me this time. (Ken loves to ask random questions that are historical, deep or silly, and all for the purpose of conversation.)

After doing a quick assessment of current events and a review of the Byzantine era, I headed to Starbucks. When I arrived, Ken was already holding court with those seated in his general vicinity. One thing I love about Ken is how he greets me. Because of some hearing loss, he is sometimes louder than others, but I love it when he says with great affection in his voice, "Oh there's my dear, dear friend Steve! Come give me a hug!" I love that!

We sat down, and he was loaded for bear, asking me about Karl Barth, the Catholic Catechism, and the Reformation. I felt like a kid taking a test, but knew that no matter what I knew or didn't know, I was still Ken's dear, dear friend.

After several minutes, he leaned closer and whispered, "I know what's going on with your family."

My heart sank again, as our family was in a difficult time of transition.

Being a pastor at a large church in a small town is no place to share your needs... trust me. Kathy and I had kept the hardship we were going through as private as possible, informing only family. How Ken found out, I still don't know.

I dropped my head in shame, but immediately Ken took me by the arm and said with sincere pain in his voice, "Oh, son, I don't want you to be embarrassed. I want to help."

What had he just called me? Had he said the s-word? Had he said "son"? Back in Chapter Fourteen, I wrote about when I was in the second grade and the principal called me "son"? I remember that day so well, because that word means more to me than a colloquialism meaning buddy or pal. The word "son" means much more to me; it means, "I belong."

For all the years that I can remember, I have secretly longed for a father. I realize and am fully aware, and more than grateful, that I am blessed to have an amazingly generous older brother, that though he picked on me, he never allowed others to. He encouraged my comedy aspirations, including writing material and paying for promotional photos. He later helped me to smile without covering my mouth with my hand. I am blessed to have a friend named Mark, whose dad, Fast Eddie, was there for me during high school. I am blessed with a father-in-law, Jerry, who taught me how to use a framing hammer with one hand.

And now I am blessed to have a spiritual father, who has shown me that I am not a loser, that I am important, and that God really does have plans for me. He's a father who plays tennis and rides bikes with me and has told me again and again that I am more than able to write (and finish) this darn book! The love, advice, encouragement, comfort, and tangible assistance my family received from Paw-Paw and La-La is beyond what I could have ever imagined.

Hold the phone. There's another promise that I forgot to mention.

Now to him who is able to do immeasurably more than all we ask or imagine, according to his power that is at work within us, to him be glory in the church and in Christ Jesus throughout all generations, for ever and ever! Amen.

—Ephesians 3:20–21

Postscript

If you're reading this, I hope it's because you made it to end without skipping ahead. But if you did, there's no shame in that! I truly hope this was worth your time, and I pray that what I shared within the pages of this book helped you identify some places where shame has hindered you or someone you know in the past, and how shame influences the way you see your future. So, in summation, you are a son. You are a daughter. You belong. You matter. You are valuable. And you are worthy.

> *Instead of your shame you will receive a double portion, and instead of disgrace you will rejoice in your inheritance. And so you will inherit a double portion in your land, and everlasting joy will be yours.*
>
> —Isaiah 61:7

This has not been easy to write, because not only have I been a recipient of shame, I have also played a role in distributing shame upon others. While sharing personal experiences, my desire was to do so carefully and without bringing reproach or shame to another. Instead of using their actual names, I most often renamed or assigned descriptions or titles to people who appear in some stories. Where I have received permission, I used their real names.

Also, there can potentially develop an unintended and unfortunate result of a book like this. It can create in any of us an overly zealous desire to make dealing with shame the next new thing, misleading us to pursue and expose shame wherever we think it might exist. Shame shouldn't become the new hot topic or focus in our Bible studies, home groups, or Sunday school classes. And I have absolutely no desire to go on a speaking tour or do conferences on shame. Our focus should always be on the relationship between a loving God and those He created in His image. Plus, I am a little concerned that writing this book could lead those who have a Bible-only mentality to wholly reject this book. I did my best to utilize Scripture appropriately and not force a verse to fit into my thinking. It would help to read this as my testimony rather than a new theology.

Something to keep in mind:

Finally, brothers and sisters, whatever is true, whatever is noble, whatever is right, whatever is pure, whatever is lovely, whatever is admirable—if anything is excellent or praiseworthy—think about such things. Whatever you have learned or received or heard from me, or seen in me—put it into practice. And the God of peace will be with you.

—Philippians 4:8–9

To those I have shamed, intentionally or unintentionally, I am truly sorrowful and sincerely ask for your forgiveness. And to those who have shamed me, I extend grace and forgiveness that is both supernatural and a choice.

Do not be afraid; you will not be put to shame. Do not fear disgrace; you will not be humiliated. You will forget the shame of your youth and remember no more the reproach of your widowhood.

—Isaiah 54:4

Bonus Chapter for Pastors, Church, and Ministry Leaders

Over my many years in ministry, I've witnessed how shame has derailed pastors and church and ministry leaders across the world. Shame is not just a western world issue, it's universal. My love for the church and its leaders has compelled me to add this (elongated) chapter because I personally know of many, many pastors and leaders who have to fight many churches' accepted view of what success is. The desire to please their congregations and produce successful results can drive a leader to spiritual bankruptcy.

In their incredibly honest and helpful book, *Overcoming the Dark Side of Leadership*, Gary L. McIntosh wrote this about his co-author Samuel D. Rema:

> *Sam discovered that an unhealthy compulsion to succeed led to a period of depression and burn-out. What was it that drove him [Sam] to work fourteen-hour days and still feel like a slacker?*[11]

I know, I know! Pick me, pick me! While McIntosh and Rema delve much deeper into this in their book, which every leader should read, I will offer a one-word answer to McIntosh's question. Yes, you guessed it: shame. Shame tells us that we are failures, that we must succeed, and that we must, must, must please our congregations and exceed every expectation. It ain't gonna happen! No leader, no matter how good he or she is, will ever accomplish what church and ministry leaders have come to expect of themselves.

Hidden shame has driven more Christian leaders into living secret and self-destructive lives than we may ever know. I have the feeling that when we read

---

11 Gary L. McIntosh and Samuel D. Rema, *Overcoming the Dark Side of Leadership* (Grand Rapids, MI: Baker Books, 2007), 13.

about fallen, high-profile Christian leaders in the headlines, there are many more suffering in silence under a veil of shame.

The way shame manifests in leaders is found in one of my favorite Jesus stories.

In the parable found in Luke 15, commonly known as The Prodigal Son, Jesus reveals three types of leadership, starting with the heart of God as portrayed by the father. The father has a loving heart, is forgiving, and is about restoring relationship.

The second leader type is the younger brother, who is about all the goodies that go with being his son but doesn't want a relationship with his father.

The third leader type is the older brother, who is all about following the rules—not because he loves the father, but to ensure he will receive his inheritance. He, too, wants the goodies and seemingly cares nothing about a relationship with his father... or his own brother.

In churches today, we seem to have mostly older and younger brother types leading churches and ministries while fewer and fewer are being led by father types. In the story, we see that the father never used shame when the younger brother returned, and neither did he use it when bringing correction to the older brother.

This bonus chapter is meant for church and ministry leaders. This is in no way meant to shame or impugn anyone's character, but to use the main characters from this well-known story as a way to understand how we tend to lead and how we might become better leaders. Let's start with the older brother first—as he would expect, I'm sure.

The Older Brother Leader

Older brother types tend to lead churches and ministries by following the letter of the law rather than the spirit of the law, and they are bent toward legalism (all law and no grace). They are not as concerned about relationships as they are focused on their goals. They are rule-followers, task-oriented, and results-driven. They rely on formulas. Success for the older brother means achieving orderly and measurable results by obeying all the rules (except the ones from which they exempt themselves).

In the parable, the older brother not only wanted what he felt was due to him, he was also incensed that his father threw a party and rejoiced that his no-good, rule-breaking brother returned after squandering what his father had given him. Older brothers have a tendency to call out or uncover the sins and mistakes of others.

Pastors and church leaders who lack compassion and understanding of scripture are in danger of acting like the older brother and lording over their congregations. If someone in their congregation repents of their sin, some pastors, instead of quietly and lovingly restoring the person, add to that person's shame by demanding that they publically confess their sin. Yes, there are some examples in Scripture concerning public acknowledgement of habitual and unrepentant sin, but this is the exception and not the rule. Lording-over leadership is steeped in a religious spirit.

So what is this religious spirit, you may ask? According to John 8, it appears to me that it is someone who is more interested in testing Jesus than genuinely being concerned about the other person's sin. The religious spirit was at work in the Pharisees, who never shied away from an opportunity to shame someone.

The incident in John 8 deals with a woman caught in an adulterous act. Notice it's only the woman who is brought before Jesus. No man is likewise accused, just her. The Pharisees are intent on publically shaming this woman and making Jesus squirm. They want to see what this gentle rabbi and lover of sinners will do when presented with an issue of the law. The only people who squirm that day were the Pharisees.

> They were using this question as a trap, in order to have a basis for accusing him.
>
> But Jesus bent down and started to write on the ground with his finger. When they kept on questioning him, he straightened up and said to them, "Let any one of you who is without sin be the first to throw a stone at her." Again he stooped down and wrote on the ground.
>
> At this, those who heard began to go away one at a time, the older ones first, until only Jesus was left, with the woman still standing there. Jesus straightened up and asked her, "Woman, where are they? Has no one condemned you?"
>
> "No one, sir," she said.
>
> "Then neither do I condemn you," Jesus declared. "Go now and leave your life of sin."
>
> —John 8:6–11

In the midst of a religiously charged atmosphere, Jesus bends down and starts doodling in the dirt. I've heard sermon after sermon about what He was writing in the dirt, and you know what? I don't care! Confession time: as a teacher, I sometimes battle a religious spirit that provokes me to desire or seek unnecessary revelation about a passage of scripture. What I do care about is what He said.

Jesus calmly doodles as the Pharisees pepper Him with question after meaningless question. He finally straightens up and says, *"Let any one of you who is without sin be the first to throw a stone at her"* (John 8:7). Awkward!

By the way, when Jesus tells her to go and sin no more, He didn't say it in a judgmental way; He said it because He knew that sin was not good for her… or for us!

The Pharisees became snared in their own trap. They set themselves up as the arbiters or spiritual police, and it all came crashing down around them. Church leaders are not, and were never intended to be, the God Squad, calling out sin and religiously correcting people.

> *To the elders among you, I appeal as a fellow elder and a witness of Christ's sufferings who also will share in the glory to be revealed: Be shepherds of God's flock that is under your care, watching over them—not because you must, but because you are willing, as God wants you to be; not pursuing dishonest gain, but eager to serve; not lording it over those entrusted to you, but being examples to the flock. And when the Chief Shepherd appears, you will receive the crown of glory that will never fade away.*
>
> *In the same way, you who are younger, submit yourselves to your elders. All of you, clothe yourselves with humility toward one another, because, "God opposes the proud but shows favor to the humble."*
>
> —1 Peter 5:1–5

Another thing that older brother types do is apply blanket rules or formulas to specific situations. Case in point, you send your son to a Christian therapist because of a struggle he has with pornography. Now, the Bible does say in Matthew 18:9, *"If your eye causes you to stumble, gouge it out…"* Would you be okay if your son came home with his eyes gouged out? Of course not! Then is it okay for a church leader to treat every person and every situation with their interpretation and application of scripture? Hmm… I think not.

I've seen some of the gentlest people blow up when I share this illustration. So before anyone stops reading and concludes that I am a heretic, let's spend a few more minutes on this.

Let me emphatically and unequivocally state that I believe the Bible, all of it. I have no desire to be a spiritual schizophrenic when it comes to the Word. If I am going to believe that an invisible God became visible, hung out with the dregs of humanity, walked on water, and healed people… was murdered, buried for three days, arose from the dead, entrusted eleven misfits with His eternal plans, and then became invisible all over again… then I can certainly believe everything else! Along with my unwavering faith that the Bible is the inerrant Word of God, I also can discern the difference between actual historical events and the parables Jesus told in order to illustrate spiritual truths. So with that established, let's soldier on.

I believe that the Ten Commandments are just that—commandments. They carry over from the Old Testament to the New Testament and Jesus affirms them in His teachings. He had no problem with the Law of Moses. What He did take issue with was the implementation of the rules of the Pharisees. Of the 613 laws of Judaism, Moses on Mount Sinai only delivered ten. 247 of them come from the Book of Leviticus. The remainder of the 613 was believed to have either been spoken and recorded in the tent of meeting or spoken at Mount Sinai and then repeated and recorded in the tent of meeting. Either way, there are a lot of laws.

God-fearing people became so intent on keeping themselves and others from breaking the Law of Moses that they created laws, or a fence, around the law so that no one would even get close to violating the law. Jesus reveals this when He declares, *"They worship me in vain; their teachings are merely human rules"* (Matthew 15:9).

In some ways, because of the heart of man, some of our rules of Christianity have simply replaced the Pharisees' rules. The modern-day church still has a tendency to rely on rules taught by men, because rules are measureable, definable, and keep things under control. Clearly defined rules allow some people to feel safe within the confines of the rules, because relying on a faith-based, love relationship with Jesus is too iffy.

That's how rules like "Don't smoke," "Don't chew," and "Don't go with girls who do" enter our collective Christian psyche. Some churches have rules that insist on men wearing ties and ladies wearing dresses to enter their sanctuaries. We fall prey to the mindset that man was made for the Sabbath, and therefore rules are created and implemented in churches that lead to birthing denominations of like-minded rule-keepers.

When Jesus spoke about gouging out one's eye or cutting off one's hand, He was using metaphoric language that everyone understood. How do we know that? Well, first, no one challenged Him or demanded to know what He meant by such a statement. The people of that time were familiar with this type of metaphoric and illustrative teaching.

Secondly, nowhere in the New Testament is there an indication that this became a practice. Paul never tells the Corinthians or Galatians, who had scores of sensual and sexual issues in the church, to hold a mass eye-gouging or hand-severing service. In fact, he deals with man's sexual desires by stating "Get married, dude," which I paraphrased earlier from 1 Corinthians 7:9.

Older brother type leaders are tempted to mold scripture into rules to fit their beliefs and convictions. I have a friend who pastors a very large church in a prominent denomination. We have similar childhood experiences, as his father (like my mother) was an alcoholic. We've laughed and cried together, sharing our childhood stories.

We share so much in common that he was shocked when I didn't share his conviction concerning the controversial topic of drinking. His stance is zero-tolerance toward alcohol of any kind. In his opinion, one beer or one glass of wine is the same as drinking a fifth of whiskey and then driving a busload of orphans to the movies.

I understand his views. My mother's battle with alcohol, and subsequent family issues, made me hate it, too. I wouldn't touch it with a ten-foot pole. And then I became a Christian and started reading the Bible. It wasn't long before I learned of Jesus' first miracle: turning water into wine. Uh-oh.

Fortunately or unfortunately for me, the little missionary church I attended, upon my conversion to Christ, held the same view I had of drinking, and it was explained to me that the wine that Jesus made was more like grape juice than fermented wine. Whew! With my personal beliefs still intact, for many years I repeated this explanation whenever I was called upon to deal with the water-in-to-wine controversy.

Fast-forward several years to when I became serious about God's Word and began *unlearning* the explanations taught by men. As I was breaking in my new-found love of the Word, I received a Hebrew/Greek Study Bible. I was intrigued how often one word in English could be a paragraph in the Greek.

I was also impressed when learning the meaning of a single word—words like *Oinos*, for instance. Merrily reading along in Ephesians 5, I came across verse 18, where Paul admonishes the church not to get drunk on "wine." But I thought the wine in the New Testament was more like grape juice! I looked at the word "wine" again, and there beside it was the number 3631. That number in my Hebrew/Greek Study Bible corresponds with a Greek word found in the Greek dictionary in the back of my beloved Study Bible. Finding the number, I discovered that the word *Oinos*, which means "strong or intoxicating drink."[12] Suddenly a chill went up my back. Honestly it did. At that moment, my thoughts turned to

---

12 Spiros Zodhiates, Th.D., ed. *Hebrew-Greek Study Bible, New American Standard Version* (Chattanooga, TN: AMG Publishers, 1990), 1860.

John 2 and my deeply held doctrine of Jesus making grape juice. I exhaled and turned to John 2, and there in verse nine was the word "wine" with a familiar number next to it… 3631.

I actually laughed out loud, because I had never made the connection in Ephesians 5:18 that if they were drinking grape juice, how were they getting drunk? And then back to John 2, what's the miracle in making grape juice? When no one is looking, you just squeeze a few grapes, add some sugar, and voila… grape juice. The miracle was in Jesus making strong, fermented, or intoxicating wine for winemaking, which is a very long process that can't be accomplished while someone's back is momentarily turned.

Now, why did I tell you all of that? Weren't we exploring the older brother type of leadership? Yes. I needed to give you that background so you will understand what comes next. My pastor friend insisted that anyone in any role of leadership in his church had signed an agreement that they would never drink alcohol of any kind. His personal beliefs and convictions about alcohol excluded and shamed mature believers from becoming leaders in the church. His views permeated the church, and there developed a division among the drinkers and non-drinkers. It often manifested when someone would be asked to consider volunteering for a leadership role, and because they had an occasional glass of wine they would nervously decline. How sad is that?

At this point, it all went south, and the church imploded. One evening, at a local restaurant, a leader from his church was spotted with a glass of wine. One of the church members called another member, and when word got to the pastor, he immediately removed this member from his leadership position. He called the person on their cell phone, while they were *still in the restaurant*. And my friend wonders why his leadership was questioned after this event.

I shared this thought with him. "You know, the Word admonished the Ephesians not to get drunk. Paul never told them they couldn't drink." I wondered if his zero-tolerance theology seeped into other aspects of discipline, so I added, "Would you advise someone in your church who has a tendency toward overeating (gluttony) to stop eating altogether?"

Another issue that older brother type leaders battle is not seeing people as they *could* be, but seeing them through the lens of their past sins or struggles. Most, if not all, pastors and church leaders know this verse, which by the way is also popular among refrigerator magnets:

Therefore, if anyone is in Christ, the new creation has come: The old has gone, the new is here!

—2 Corinthians 5:17

Interestingly, verse 16 is not as memorized and rarely makes an appearance on the refrigerator magnet circuit. We are even given a hint that we should read verse 16 because of the first word in 17—the word "therefore." I learned in Sunday school that whenever you see the word "therefore" the simple rule of thumb is, "What's that therefore, there for?" Well, here's what that therefore was there for:

So from now on we regard no one from a worldly point of view. Though we once regarded Christ in this way, we do so no longer.

—2 Corinthians 5:16

Older brother leaders are not prone to seeing people with the eyes of the spirit (Ephesians 1), but rather through the eyes of their flesh—or better said, through their opinions and experiences. One of the greatest prophets in all of Scripture, Samuel, needed to have his eyes refocused when God spoke to him concerning who would be the next King of Israel.

What's troubling is that older brother types are often natural leaders, but shame can dull their God-given gifts and talents. They don't view things through God's eyes, but through the eyes of self-reliance and personal success. This often results in them treating their congregations like cows and driving them like a cattle rancher rather than seeing them as sheep who need to be led by a shepherd. Many times the mindset becomes, "Come hell or high water, *my* church is going to get to where we are supposed to be going!"

Shame has twisted many pastors of churches into becoming more like CEOs of corporations. Their identity becomes lost in the ABCs of church management—attendance, buildings, and cash—so they don't have time to waste on sheep who don't keep up, and they quickly lose their patience with them. This mindset invades the pulpit, and their messages become more about honoring authority and embracing their vision rather than *"strengthening, encouraging, and [providing] comfort"* (1 Corinthians 14:3).

If only older brother type leaders would model their leadership style after Jesus. Something I find fascinating is that Jesus "slow-walked" His disciples. He never ran ahead of them, and He only once asserted His authority by making them get in a boat, after feeding the four thousand. Jesus was direct but gentle with His disciples. When we see Jesus speak harshly in the New Testament, He is not speaking to the disciples. When He said things like *"[this] unbelieving generation"* (Mark 9:19), He was speaking to the spirit of the generation. When speaking to His disciples, it's as if He were speaking to little boys. He says things like, "Why did you have so little faith?" Notice in Mark 9:33–37 that when the disciples had the audacity to argue among themselves about who the greatest was, Jesus didn't get mad at them for wanting to be great; He simply defined heaven's perception of what greatness is. Unfortunately, older brothers seem more interested in behavior modification than heart transformation.

The Younger Brother Leader

The younger brother type of leadership relies heavily on feelings, intuition, and sensitivity toward others. They are more focused on relationships than results. Now, this may sound much better than the older brother, but there are still problems with this type of leadership, as it tends toward humanism. Humanism is all grace, but no law. Younger brother types often defer to the feelings and pulse of their congregation rather than honoring the purposes and precepts of God.

As the older brother is often a natural leader, the younger brother is often a natural pastor. They typically score well in emotional intelligence and have a good measure of compassion and empathy. But their own shame can take all this good and twist them into approval-seeking, man-pleasing cruise directors. Their desire to be loved and accepted will prevent them from making decisions as they lead by committee. Like the prodigal son, they would rather party to the approval of their friends than honor the wishes of their father. They are fearful of rejection, so they tend to preach messages about tolerance and acceptance and avoid any messages that address the sin nature of man. Though they would never dream of driving their sheep like cattle, they can frustrate their flock, because they never seem to go anywhere.

King Saul is an example of the kind of person a younger brother leader battles. In 1 Samuel 9, we learn that Saul was an impressive young man without an equal and a head taller than his peers or relatives (9:2). Saul was considerate of his father (9:5) and humble (9:21). But somewhere during his rule as king, he became unimpressive, inconsiderate of his heavenly Father, and weak-willed. There is strength in true humility before God. Saul turned away from remaining humble before God and turned toward the approval of men. What younger brothers cannot abide is being disliked, rejected, or minimized. Their battle with shame will provoke them to jump through hoops and dance to everyone else's favorite tune. They will even accept being totally disrespected, as long as they will be accepted. Younger brothers often get into trouble because they cannot say the word "No."

Issues from their past will often make them feel compelled to outrun who they are (or were) and create a new self-image rather than allowing God to restore and reshape them as He sees fit. Jeremiah 18:1–5 tells of how God desires to shape and mold us, like clay in a potter's hand. Younger brother types can appear to be loving and helpful while their true desire is really to be loved and helped themselves. It's not unusual for these type of leaders to advocate for the downtrodden and impoverished and never realize their mixed motives.

Older brothers will lock themselves away, spending hours in research preparing a great Sunday sermon, but not make the time to visit with or tend to the members of their church. Conversely, younger brothers will spend all of their time visiting and tending to their flock and show up on Sunday unprepared, offering up a shoot-from-the-hip message, mostly derived from movies or pop culture. Both need to find time for both. As King Solomon wrote in Ecclesiastics 7:18, *"It is good to grasp one and not let go of the other. Whoever fears God will avoid all extremes."*

Desiring to be a godly leader, I've seen many younger brothers twist in the ever-changing winds of their congregations' expectations and opinions of where, how, and when the church is to proceed. They dance as fast as they can and run from fire to fire, attempting to please everyone except the Lord they serve. Meanwhile, older brothers excuse themselves from interacting with church members believing that their time is best utilized isolated in study and devotion to God's Word. This results in a well-crafted message of information that doesn't connect with their congregation. When challenged, they can become lone rangers of the faith, and as a result they won't tolerate any suggestions or correction and refuse to entertain any counsel but their own. The younger brother may have the affection of his congregation, but though his messages are heartfelt, they are hard to follow. When challenged, they can become hyper-spiritual and mask their lack of preparation by saying, "I want to challenge you to rely on the Holy Spirit, like I do."

So in their attempt to be godly leaders, both older and younger brother leaders need to realize that the word "godliness" in 2 Peter 1:6 means "to look both ways." Not like before you cross a street, but to look toward God and then toward men. True righteousness means that not only is a person in right relationship with God, they become right in relationship with others. To look both ways means that we correctly worship God as we correctly serve others. Jesus let us know that we can incorrectly worship Him by drawing near to Him with our lips, while having our hearts far away from Him (Matthew 15:8). We can also incorrectly serve others by giving them what we want to give rather than what they need (Luke 11:11).

Both the older brother and younger brother leader have triggers that can potentially provoke a shame attack. One trigger they have in common is when someone decides to leave their church. It upsets them both, but for different reasons. The older brother calculates how their leaving will affect the church budget and their level of influence on other givers. The younger brother interprets leaving as rejection and worries that others may reject him, too. In these scenarios, both the older and younger brother usually damage the person or family who leaves.

Remember, shame always wants to pay it forward. I've seen leaders question people's salvation, maturity, and even their sanity when they attempt to leave their church. In doing this, they create a culture of fear and intimidation that controls people from leaving their church. Once shame is deployed, the collective mindset becomes, "If you want to leave our church, there must be something wrong with you!" Shame has been used to control individuals and families in churches for generations.

But there is good news. Every older brother and younger brother has the potential to become a healthy pastor and leader. Instead of leading in a way that encourages church members to *"take hold of that for which Christ Jesus took hold of [them]"* (Philippians 3:12), they warehouse the beloved and expect them to come to hear them preach and enjoy the worship show each and every Sunday.

The Fatherly Leader

Looking back over the last generation, I have observed that churches tended to choose the brother types rather than the father type to lead their congregations. In my view, it started around the late 1970s when churches began hiring young men to pastor the youth in congregations all across America.

It became common practice, and then the norm, for a young man fresh out of Bible college or seminary to be hired as a youth pastor, before getting his chance at being called up to the "big leagues" of being a senior pastor. What churches often ended up with were older and younger brother type leaders who had no desire to work with youth, but were required to put in their time as a youth pastor first.

Imagine the unintended shame this caused both youth pastors and the youth they were hired to serve. Prior to this, parents bore the responsibility to train their children in the nurturing and admonition of the Lord. Suddenly a new idea was hatched that churches needed someone "cool" to lead the youth and thereby show that following Jesus was "cool." I've got some bad news for some of you: following Jesus will never be culturally cool. And if it ever does become cool, rest assured that the message of the Gospel will have been watered down.

Youth pastors by nature (I apologize in advance) tend to have a know-it-all, I'm-going-to-change-the-world mentality coming out of Bible college or seminary. They have spent the last four years learning about the ups and downs of church history and have a quiver full of messages ready to place on the string of their bows and fire them off into an unsuspecting congregation.

But before they ever have a chance to preach on a Sunday, they have to plan camps and retreats, oversee an anemic youth budget, endure lock-ins, manage Sunday School teachers who are old enough to be their grandparents, submit to a pastor who may never have served as a youth pastor, and battle their own immaturity and lack of life experience... all while "leading" a group of students who are just a few years younger. This can all lead to an insurmountable amount of frustration, and yes, shame—a shame which brings about the feeling that they can't do anything right.

Then there's the added shame when others in the church feel that youth pastors are not ready or good enough to preach on Sunday. And where do you think the blessing of shame paid forward goes? The youth. Unless the church has a plan in place to mentor these young men and women who serve in our youth ministries, we will continue to groom older and younger brother type pastors.

Now, I'm not saying you should fire your youth staff. That horse has already left the stable. What I'm suggesting is that we take an objective look at how we view our pastors and how they may view themselves. It's not that difficult to discern how pastors views themselves—just listen to the topics upon which they tend to preach and how they act in social settings and when they're not on the platform. I have already given a non-comprehensive, very broad brushstroke of older and younger brother type leaders to allow room for nuances of individual leaders, who may have a combination of the aforementioned tendencies.

When an older or younger brother type becomes a senior pastor, they usually bring with them the tendencies they had as a youth pastor or as the senior pastor of their previous church. It takes a wise and patient group of elders, deacons, or church leaders to recognize and restore these brother types.

What father type leaders bring to the church is much different than that which the modern church has grown accustomed. They bring stability and a sense that God is in charge. They are there to teach, instruct, correct, rebuke, mentor, and lead with great patience and gobs of love.

Healthy fathers never shame their children, and they never try to control them. A lot of shame is dispensed when we try to control others, because it sends a message that says, "You don't know what you're doing, and so I'll be your brain and conscience for you."

When the prodigal son came to his father and asked for his inheritance, to do with as he saw fit, the father gave it to him, no strings attached. You see, the father had already set aside something he was unconditionally going to give his son. The Pharisees were aghast at this, because in their traditions, if a son had done this, he would have been put to death. But the father gave what he had planned to give and let his rebellious son leave and live the life he chose.

Unhealthy fathers (this goes for mothers, too) are unable to let adult children live the lives they choose. Granted, if the son in Luke 15 were a boy, I'm sure the story would have included a paddle and someone being sent to bed without their supper. The younger brother, though young, was a man—a man who had made up his mind to live as he saw fit and asked for what he knew was apportioned to him. When pastors lead like the father, they don't insist that their members attend church every Sunday. They don't use guilt or manipulation to get members to volunteer or sign up for various workdays on the church grounds. And when someone decides to leave their church, they don't automatically try to convince them to stay. They gently and appropriately inquire, without intruding, about the reasons why. If they've failed the member, they ask for forgiveness; if the person is leaving for the wrong reasons, they gently encourage them that as they leave, to leave well. If they are leaving because they feel they are being led to or better fed at another church, father type leaders approve and bless their decision.

I imagine that right about this point, some who are reading this are getting angry enough to stop reading, throw this book in the trash (I'd rather you return it and get your money back), or head to your computer to fire off a blistering email to me. So, which are you—the older or younger brother? I'm just asking. Please stay with me for a few more paragraphs, then you can do whatever you decide to do with this book.

In churches today, we seem to have scores of adult-adolescents piling up in the pews. These adult-adolescents are people who carry around a burden of shame which inhibits or prohibits them from making their own decisions. They need someone to tell them what to do, and sadly, there are more than enough adult-adolescent pastors who feed off this and medicate their own shame. They need followers so they can outrun their own shame, and they are more than willing to tell others what to do. These pastors don't teach; they tell. They don't encourage their members to go further; they create and foster a dependency on their leadership and ministry. The father in Luke 15 said, "Here's your stuff. I'll be here if you need me."

Over time, among their congregations, older and younger brother leadership will begin to breed frustration, mistrust, and resentment for the very things they used to require from their pastors. Seemingly without warning, church members, burdened with their own shame, will revolt and push back on their leadership. That's when the shame hits the fan. The church starts showing signs of fracturing and then begins to split. It's not long before the church will implode or explode. Families become divided and lifelong friends refuse to speak to each other, as the shrapnel of shame wounds anyone in its path. How do I know this? I have the t-shirt.

There appear, again and again, consistent patterns in our human culture. There is the pattern of fads and fashion. What's in is soon to be out, and what was once out will make its reappearance and be embraced as retro. Be assured, retro will soon be out again, too. There is also a pendulum pattern. What one generation rebels against, the next will embrace. Church culture is no different. We argue over hymns versus contemporary worship and hymnals versus PowerPoint.

A generation ago, pastors had three points and a poem and would preach expository sermons. In our recent past and current culture, pastors regale congregations with practical and relatable messages using movie clips, song lyrics, pop culture references, and hire designers to create stage sets complete with 3D props to emphasize their sermon series. That was so cool… for a while.

What unfortunately begins to happen in many churches is that there's so much effort and time spent creating these incredible stage sets that the message becomes secondary. Soon the very thing that attracted people to a particular church becomes an irritant and distraction. And suddenly people want expository teaching, to hear an old hymn, and all those Bible stories don't seem to be so boring anymore.

Healthy fathers never make good stories boring. Fathers have a way of fostering an appreciation for things and instilling gratitude. Though they are not easily impressed with the latest fad, they will find what's good and utilize it. They aren't controlled by change, but they aren't against it, either. The prodigal son's request could have heaped shame upon the father, who could have ruminated about all the mistakes he made raising his son. He could have easily thought, *My son wants all the stuff that goes with being my child, but he wants nothing to do with me.* That must have hurt deeply, yet the father knew his son's request had *nothing* to do with the way he parented him.

Let me give you some odd equations that you may have noticed in your own sphere of relationships:

- Bad parenting sometimes equates to ending up with great kids.
- Great parenting sometimes equates to ending up with bad kids.
- In summation: free will is alive and well!

A lot of parents take too much blame for their children's failures and too much credit for their successes. Older and younger brother leaders have the same tendency. Healthy fathers (and mothers) allow their children to make mistakes and also give room for them to learn from the consequences of their choices.

The father in Luke 15 never shamed the younger brother's decision to leave, but allowed him the freedom to leave and experience the life he chose, all while knowing what consequences those choices would bring. Once the son came to his senses, he surely felt ashamed of his actions and the way he had treated his father. Believing he was unfit to be a son, he returned home in hopes of becoming an employee. When his father welcomed him home, even though he had sinned, the father's loving acceptance transformed what could have easily been shame into sorrow—for it is sorrow that leads us to repentance. Shame leads a person to deeper and darker places of loneliness and isolation, with no hope of redemption.

The father not only had to deal with his younger son's shame, he had to address his older son's propensity to shame others. The older brother was furious with his brother, but even more so with his father. He was angry for his brother's immature and selfish actions and even angrier at his father's display of loving acceptance and forgiveness for his wayward brother.

Notice the conversation between them. The older brother says to the father, *"But when this son of yours who has squandered your property with prostitutes comes home, you kill the fattened calf for him!"* (Luke 15:30). Now look at the father's response to his older son: *"But we had to celebrate and be glad, because this brother of yours was dead and is alive again; he was lost and is found"* (Luke 15:32). The older brother is not only unforgiving of his brother, he tries to shame his father for doing so.

By the way, this part really irritated the Pharisees, because they knew Jesus was referring to them, as the older brother.

When fathers lead churches, there is a greater measure of stability, maturity, and hopefulness instilled in the congregation. Fathers are reluctant to react; they respond. Fathers don't fret about issues; they pray and seek wise counsel. And fathers are more interested in looking for the treasure buried within a person, rather than focusing or commenting on the dirt that covers the yet-to-be-revealed treasure inside someone. Fathers think and behave like beloved sons and treat others the same.

All too often, the older/younger brothers think like orphans and treat others as they see themselves—as fundamentally flawed people unworthy of God's grace, and therefore they must earn the right to come back home after making poor decisions. When the younger brother returns to his father wearing the iron coat of shame, his father lifts it off by reminding him that he is still his son and gives him a new garment to wear. Thank God that a father leaves the porch light burning and a key under the mat.

In summation, the father (God) represents the way pastors (and fathers) are to lead. The father helps the older brother (the Pharisees), who is only concerned with rules, see his younger brother (sinners), who is only concerned with grace, in a different light while at the same time helping the younger brother (sinners) see himself in a different light. When the older brother (the Pharisees) refers to his brother (sinners) as "your son" (the problem), the father gently reminds him that he's "your brother" (the reason we need a Savior).

A good father knows that we need both the law and the grace of God, who is our Rock and our Redeemer.

One More Thing

So much of our world's system is whacked beyond belief and common sense. We have a culture that celebrates broken people. It's so self-focused that people will spend years and millions of dollars trying to become people they are not. Consider the recent revelations of Bruce Jenner and Rachel Dolezal (the Caucasian woman who self-identifies as black). In the immortal words of Yukon Cornelius, "It isn't a fit night for man or beast!"

When all that we have relied or depended on for security (job, talent, relationships) gets swept out from under us, we tend to sink rather than swim… when, in fact, we are invited to walk on the very water that seemingly seeks to pull us under. I know firsthand that no one drowns gracefully. We kick and thrash and scream bloody murder when we feel the waves overtaking us, and then we will accept help from wherever we can get it.

Sometimes in moments of utter desperation and fear, all we have to do is stand up. So often we are drowning in waist-deep water. What feels so real and overwhelming is just that… a feeling. Over the last few years I've been learning that though feelings are very real, they can also be wrong. When we are drowning, we second-guess and criticize everything we did and every decision we made that got us into the water in the first place. We can look back and easily see the mistakes we made and agonize over what we now see as a lack of wisdom or common sense.

But we must remember that hindsight is always 20/20. When looking back and thinking we woulda-coulda-shoulda done something, we need to recognize that we made those choices and decisions based on the information and wisdom we had at the time!

So many people revert to coping when things don't go as they planned or thought they should go. Coping is what leads to a hardened heart. Jesus said,

"Blessed are those who mourn, for they will be comforted" (Matthew 5:4). That comfort is to come from the Lord and not from us. Comfort comes from the Comforter, who calls us from deep to deep. Coping comes from our own strength and can lead us to cynicism and unbelief.

Hopefully, dear reader, you have more wisdom, more life experience, more humility, and a greater dependency upon the Giver of All Things. The world, broken as it is, is your oyster! Don't settle for a baloney sandwich when the King of all kings and Lord of all lords is offering you a steak. What are your dreams? What makes your heart beat faster? What activity or mission connects you to Jesus more than anything else? That's the lane you are to run in:

> *Therefore, since we are surrounded by such a great cloud of witnesses, let us throw off everything that hinders and the sin that so easily entangles. And let us run with perseverance the race marked out for us, fixing our eyes on Jesus, the pioneer and perfecter of faith. For the joy set before him he endured the cross, scorning its shame, and sat down at the right hand of the throne of God. Consider him who endured such opposition from sinners, so that you will not grow weary and lose heart.*
>
> —Hebrews 12:1–3

So I encourage you to get in your lane and run your leg of the race.

Appendix

Identifying Shame

Are you aware when shame entered your life? Are you aware of areas where shame has a foothold in your life? Are you aware of why shame continues to take hold of you?

Below are some of the ways that shame enters our lives. We need to recognize and address these areas in order to become shame less.

- Unconfessed sin:
    when we have sinned.
    when others have sinned against us.
- Lack of forgiveness:
    toward ourselves.
    toward others.
- Expectations:
    Others' expectations of us.
    Our own expectations of us.
    Our expectations of others.
- Abuse:
    Mental.
    Emotional.
    Verbal.
    Physical.
    Sexual.
    Spiritual.

- Embarrassment:
    - Embarrassments *of* our own doing.
    - Embarrassments *from* another's doing.
- Life failures:
    - Bankruptcy.
    - Job loss or demotions.
    - Divorce.
- Lack of self-acceptance:
    - Physical appearance.
    - Intelligence.
    - Talent.
    - Social status.

To help put words to how shame makes us feel, below are some feelings commonly associated with shame. Do you feel:

- Belittled?
- Betrayed?
- Blamed?
- Condemned?
- Despised?
- Disgraced?
- Inferior?
- Insignificant?
- Like a loser?
- Marginalized?
- Like a mistake?
- Misunderstood?
- Overlooked?
- Stupid?
- Unacceptable?
- Unlovable?
- Unworthy?
- Worthless?

Now that you've identified some of your feelings and the areas in your life where shame has taken hold, it's time to act on what you've been reading. Shame doesn't simply leave us because it's been uncovered; it only leaves when we command it to. We have authority through Jesus to command spirits to depart from us, but we also need a replacement strategy.

When an impure spirit comes out of a person, it goes through arid places seeking rest and does not find it. Then it says, "I will return to the house I left." When it arrives, it finds the house swept clean and put in order. Then it goes and takes seven other spirits more wicked than itself, and they go in and live there. And the final condition of that person is worse than the first.

—Luke 11:24–26

When we command shame to leave, we in essence clean our spiritual house, but we also need to make sure that we don't leave our spiritual house empty; otherwise the gains we make will be short-term and harder to win back if lost again. Think about people who lose weight only to gain it back because they stopped dieting. They never really changed their eating habits. Likewise, we need to change our thinking habits rather than saying a prayer and forgetting about it.

Along with the scriptures that I've used in the book, below are some additional verses and sections of scripture for you to look up for yourself and commit them to memory. This will help keep your newly cleaned spiritual house occupied and not empty.

- Psalm 1:1–6
- Psalm 23:1–6
- Galatians 3:26–29
- Galatians 5:22–23
- Ephesians 1:17–23
- Ephesians 2:6–10
- Ephesians 6:10–18
- Philippians 4:4–9
- Philippians 4:13
- Philippians 4:19
- Colossians 3:1–4
- Colossians 3:12–17

Shameless

- 1 Thessalonians 5:23–24
- 2 Timothy 1:6–7
- 2 Timothy 1:12
- Hebrews 12:1–3

Recommended Reading

Dr. Henry Cloud, *Necessary Endings* (New York, NY: Harper Collins, 2010).

Dr. Henry Malone, *Shame-Identity Thief* (Irving, TX: Vision Life Publications, 2006).

Don Crossland, *A Journey toward Wholeness* (Nashville, TN: StarSong Publishing, 1991).

Dr. Henry Cloud and Dr. John Townsend, *Boundaries* (Grand Rapids, MI: Zondervan, 1992).

Dr. Gary Chapman, *The Five Love Languages* (Chicago, IL: Moody Publishers, 1995).

Emerson Eggerichs, *Love and Respect* (Brentwood, TN: Integrity Publishers, 2004).

Gary L. McIntosh & Samuel D. Rema, *Overcoming the Dark Side of Leadership* (Grand Rapids, MI: Baker Books, 2007).